Animals in Spirit

Animals in Spirit

Our faithful companions' transition to the afterlife

Penelope Smith

ATRIA BOOKS
New York London Toronto Sydney

BEYOND WORDS
PUBLISHING

ATRIA BOOKS
A Division of Simon & Schuster, Inc.
1230 Avenue of the Americas
New York, NY 10020

BEYOND WORDS
PUBLISHING
20827 N.W. Cornell Road, Suite 500
Hillsboro, Oregon 97124-9808
503-531-8700 / 503-531-8773 fax
www.beyondword.com

Editors: Julie Steigerwaldt and Jessica Bryan
Managing editor: Lindsay S. Brown
Proofreader: Jennifer Weaver-Neist
Cover design: Carol Sibley and Sara E. Blum
Interior design: Sara E. Blum
Composition: William H. Brunson Typography Services

First Atria Books/Beyond Words trade paperback edition January 2008

ATRIA BOOKS and colophon are trademarks of Simon & Schuster, Inc.
Beyond Words Publishing is a division of Simon & Schuster, Inc.

For more information about special discounts for bulk purchases,
please contact Simon & Schuster Special Sales at 1-800-456-6798 or
business@simonandschuster.com.

Manufactured in the United States of America

10 9 8 7 6 5 4 3 2 1

Library of Congress Cataloging-in-Publication Data
Smith, Penelope.
    Animals in spirit : our faithful companions' transition to the afterlife / Penelope Smith.
        p.   cm.
    1. Pet owners—Psychology.   2. Pets—Death—Psychological aspects.   3. Bereavement—
Psychological aspects.   4. Human-animal communication.   5. Extrasensory perception
in animals.   6. Telepathy.   I. Title.

SF411.47.S65   2008
155.9'37—dc22
                                                                                    2007016258

ISBN-13: 978-1-58270-177-6
ISBN-10:   1-58270-177-6

The corporate mission of Beyond Words Publishing, Inc.: *Inspire to Integrity*

This book is dedicated to the joy of sharing life on Earth with spirit in a multitude of forms— animal, plant, mineral, elemental—in the great tapestry of Nature supporting us harmoniously through life and death.

Contents

Acknowledgments   ix

Introduction   xi

1   Animal Awareness of Life and Death   1

2   Human Influence and the Dying Process   7

3   Letting Go and Euthanasia   25

4   Animal Choice and Purpose   41

5   Shelter and Rescued Animals   63

6   Dimensions of the Spirit Realm   71

7   Guilt and Grieving   81

8   Messages from Departed Animals   107

9   Animals Returning   133

10 Contacting Your Animal Friend in Spirit   167

11 Identity, Individuality, and Oneness   171

Contributors   180

Acknowledgments

Thank you to all the wonderful people who contributed their heart-felt experiences in communicating with their animal friends who are dying or who have left this world. We hold in our hearts and souls the greatest respect, love, and appreciation for our beloved animal companions, who assist us on our mutual journeys—in body and in spirit—with love and blessings as our eternal guides and friends.

Introduction

A child replied to an adult who wondered aloud why animal lives are shorter than human lives: *Everybody is born so they can learn how to live a good life loving everybody and being nice. Animals already know how to do this, so they don't have to stay as long.*

All of us who have the privilege of intimately sharing life with animals will have to face the eventual death of the animal companions who are dear to us. When people remember how to communicate mind-to-mind, heart-to-heart, and soul-to-soul with their animal friends in life, it can bridge a gap, making the emotionally wrenching time of animal departure from the physical realm a more peaceful and even enriching experience.

When the first edition of my book on the subject of communicating with animals, *Animal Talk*, appeared in 1978, only a few animal communicators were practicing professionally worldwide. Now, hundreds of animal communicators are helping people bridge the gap. Millions have learned about the subject of telepathic communication with animals through publications and courses. Books, audio and video recordings, training programs, articles, and radio and television programs are available to help people remember their innate ability, make the connection, and understand what animals are communicating. When it comes to facing the death of our animal companions, it can help enormously to be prepared in this way.

The intention of this book is to help you transform your experience of the cycle of life and death of your animal friends into food for your soul. As animals make their transition from the physical into the spiritual realm, we can be strengthened by feeling their presence deep in our hearts as we learn to accept and understand the full experience. Our animal companions can be forever friends for us if we continue to communicate with them and recognize who they really are.

Animals in Spirit offers a concentrated overview of the subject and includes a variety of stories and insights that can be applied to your own relationships with animals. The stories in this book are derived from communicating with many animals of diverse species. These are direct experiences from animals, communicated by them to me, to other animal communicators, and to their human companions who have requested help in their animal friends' transition from life to death and beyond. My wish is that you will be encouraged to communicate with your departed animal friends and tend the embers of your heart and soul connection beyond the physical form, so the fire of love can grow and become a constant inspiration in your life.

Thank you for embarking on this journey into the minds, hearts, and the very souls of our animal friends, exploring how our intimate connection with them extends from life to death and beyond.

> *Do not stand at my grave and weep.*
> *I am not there. I do not sleep.*
>
> *I am a thousand winds that blow.*
> *I am the diamond glints on snow.*
> *I am the sun on ripened grain.*
> *I am the gentle autumn rain.*
>
> *When you awake in morning's hush,*
> *I am the swift uplifting rush*
> *Of quiet birds in circled flight.*
> *I am the stars that shine at night.*
>
> *Do not stand at my grave and cry.*
> *I am not there. I did not die.*

—Author unknown

1

The physical body can be thought of as old clothing that we take off and leave behind as our spirit walks through death's doorway. When our spirit reaches the other side of the doorway, it's alive, conscious, and ready for a different kind of life. As one orange tabby cat put it, "Death is really no big deal. But sometimes we get very attached to our clothing."

—Jacquelin Smith, author of *Animal Communication:*
Our Sacred Connection

🐾 SPIRITUAL NATURE 🐾

In my experience communicating with thousands of animals throughout my life, and since I began counseling work as an animal communication specialist in 1971, I find that animals of all kinds are like humans—individual, conscious, spiritual beings who animate physical form. They have intelligence, mental capacities, feelings, and sensitivity—often far exceeding human awareness or expectations—that is well-suited for their purposes and functioning in the natural order of life on Earth. Communicating with animals who are "in spirit" is similar to communicating with animals who are "in body" because animals are aware of their continuous existence beyond death.

Unlike many humans in our western culture, most nonhuman animals have a sense of their spiritual nature and recognize that their physical bodies are but temporary homes. This awareness gives them an acceptance of life and death as a natural and ever-flowing cycle.

1

While they may grieve the loss of a loved one as humans do and may not wish to leave their bodies at certain times or under certain conditions, they are not socially conditioned by members of their own species to think of physical death as a horrible end or something to dread. They know that death is a transition to another state of being, like a change of costume in a play or a different way of being alive. They generally grieve their loved ones and move with the flow of life as it presents itself in each moment.

The following is an illustration of how animals feel and demonstrate the loss of their loved ones (from spring 2005 "Trunklines," a publication of The Elephant Sanctuary in Tennessee [www.elephants.com]).

Keeper records noted that on the night before [ailing Asian elephant] Lota's death, the elephants in the main barn, which is adjacent to the quarantined barn, engaged in a group ritual that had never before been documented. All of the elephants were inside the barn with outside access if they desired. Without any obvious provocation Jenny and Shirley began to roar. Simultaneously, all of the elephants lent their voices to the chorus, which built in volume and vibration until it became deafening. From one end of the barn to the other, the walls shook and the air quaked as the elephants' bellows increased to a deafening level. This display lasted for six full minutes. Each time the volume began to wane, it would then suddenly begin to build again, resembling a mass wailing display of grief.

The elephants' physical behavior throughout was curious. They all remained fairly still, standing in place yet exploding with the most profoundly emotional verbal display imaginable. As abruptly as the display began, it ended with only residual signs and guttural rumbles as the entire herd returned to its usual routine of napping, eating, and interacting.

🐾 DEATH AS PART OF LIFE 🐾

Humans in tribal societies—who live close to nature and revere the earth and its cycles—usually accept death, like birth, as part of the whole. They are aware that they continue as spirits and that there are spiritual realms or dimensions beyond the physical plane. Death is not dreaded but is often welcomed as a healthy change or even a joyous occasion to join their ancestors or dwell with the gods or spirits in other dimensions. Without this awareness and sense of the spiritual nature of animals, including ourselves, people can feel lost or experience their animal friends' departures with devastating hopelessness. A more positive emotional experience is possible when we can relish a tender continuance of connection with our animal friends.

Animals who have had a full, rich life with humans appreciate being able to share the joys and trials of their lives with us, even when they know their body is failing. Animal communicator Joanna Seere tells how she assisted in the departure of Tuskers, a twenty-six-year-old quarter horse who came to the horse sanctuary where she was teaching:

Tuskers and his best friend, Jimmy, a big thoroughbred, shared a pasture together at a beautiful horse sanctuary that I used to visit. Tuskers had come to the sanctuary to retire. One day, Tuskers was struck suddenly by terrible pain. He asked me to get help for him from the vet. Tuskers communicated to me that he felt that he had a long, good life even though it was a hard one. He said that his body felt very weak and frail and the pain in his gut was taking his breath away. The vet tried everything he could, but Tuskers' belly kept swelling and his pain kept increasing.

Tuskers asked to be released from his body. He said goodbye to his friend Jimmy as they sniffed each other for the last time. When the vet administered the injection, Tusker's spirit lifted out of his body long before the injection was finished. Jimmy gave a whinny of goodbye, turned his back on Tusker's body, and began to graze.

In the middle of the night, I was awakened by the sound of a horse galloping on the paved driveway by the farmhouse and down the street. All of the horses at the sanctuary were whinnying and racing back and forth at the fence lines of their paddocks. We all ran out of the farmhouse looking for the horse who had somehow gotten out of the field. There was no horse to be found in the driveway or on the road. All the horses were in their fields and the fence lines were intact. In a moment it became clear to me that it was Tuskers giving his final victory gallop around the farm!

For people who cultivate knowledge of and communication with spiritual dimensions beyond the physical senses, death is a change in state or viewpoint. For those who think of themselves as only their physical form, death becomes an annulment of being, an end of participation in life, and something to be avoided for as long as possible. We can learn from other species to accept death as a part of and a continuance of life.

Practicing the principles and techniques of animal communication can help you stretch into the experience of listening to animals, experiencing their feelings, and engaging in a dialogue that keeps you actively connected with your animal friends throughout the process of dying, death, and beyond. Instead of being a puzzled or devastated onlooker, you can enter into a state of spiritual communion with your animal companion that uplifts and enlightens your life.

🐾 SURVIVAL INSTINCTS 🐾

All animals, including humans, have an innate instinct or deep desire to survive and avoid dangers that could lead to injury or death. However, fearful contemplation of death is usually alien to animals in a natural setting. Wild animals often go off by themselves to die, to be taken by a predator or the elements. They do this to avoid attracting predators, who might endanger the survival of the other pack members. Healthy members of the group may also abandon or drive out an animal who is ill or injured, and not getting better, in order to protect the rest of the group from predators. This pattern remains in some domesticated animals. I have seen groups of dogs, and also chickens, attack and try to push away or kill those who are injured. While they have no predators to worry about in domesticity, the sense of danger causes them to act on these primal instincts.

Most individual domestic animals do not react in this way. Besides the innate group survival patterns, they also have the security of human protection. Many human actions are likewise motivated by hormonal, emotional, or survival promptings. In our dealings with animals of any type, including other humans, we can reason with them but always have to consider the other influences or patterns that are part of their makeup.

There is an understanding about survival needs in the natural order, and most deaths among nonhuman animals are swift and relatively painless. Wild animals are geared to leave their physical bodies when they are first caught. They do not usually experience much pain or emotional trauma in their natural, agreed-upon predator/prey relationships, and they often immediately seek another body of the same species to begin their lives anew.

Being a prey animal may not be an easy life, but it's not accompanied by the horror of the torturous, confusing, and fear-filled preludes to slaughter that are common with the current human methods of killing animals in factory farming or laboratory experiments.

Once, in his many runs through field and forest, I saw my Afghan hound, Pasha, catch a squirrel. Pasha backed up and told the squirrel, "Run, run," but the squirrel was frozen in fear, the spirit having left its body because he believed he was about to die. When the squirrel realized that his body was still alive and whole, he came out of shock, returned to his body, and ran toward a tree, bringing Pasha the joy of the chase he wanted.

🐾 EVERYONE IS EATEN 🐾

When I was teaching communication with animals in Switzerland, I received an important insight from a rabbit about the nature of death of all animals, including humans. Our group was practicing communication exercises on a dairy farm, which also had a barn full of horses in stalls and many rabbit hutches.

I was standing next to a large rabbit hutch, admiring the beauty of the gold-colored rabbit inside and how comfortable she looked in her ample bed of hay. I assumed the rabbits here were companion rabbits when I first saw the large wood hutches that housed them. Then I realized by the number of hutches and placement in the barn that these rabbits were being raised for meat. I was uncomfortable with the idea that these beautiful rabbits were going to be killed for human consumption. I decided to ask the rabbit across from me how she felt about her situation.

She looked at me and commented directly: "I have a good life here. I have good company with other rabbits nearby [and the] horses, birds, cows, humans, and other animals who visit the barn. I'm fed well and given plenty of fresh hay for a nice comfortable bed. The sun shines on me, and I get to look across the fields at the cows and sky. I am connected to my wild rabbit cousins and know what a hard life they have compared to me, always having to be wary for predators about to pounce. I am happy with my life, and I am treated well until my death."

I asked the rabbit how she felt about being raised to be eaten by humans. What she answered took me by surprise.

"We all get eaten," she said. "The horses here, the cows, even you. Everyone is eaten."

I was puzzled by her answer and told her, "My body will not get eaten by anyone. I will not be slaughtered for food as you and the other animals are."

To this she answered, "Oh yes you will. Everyone is eaten. What matters is that you enjoy your life until your death."

Then I realized what she meant. In the end, all bodies are food to nurture other species or forms of life in the great recycling center of Earth. We are all part of the web of life, which includes death and decay. Our bodies return to the Earth. My body will be eaten by worms and other small creatures, and decompose in the soil or be burned into ash that gets utilized by others for the continuance of life. None of us are exempt from being eaten or recycled through other bodies into other forms of life. As this wonderful rabbit teacher had told me, *"What matters is that you enjoy your life until your death."*

2

Human Influence and the Dying Process

The love of an animal permits us to unfold, to open up, [to] drop our defenses, and to be naked, not only physically but psychologically and spiritually as well. With an animal, we let ourselves be seen instead of hiding behind our personalities, our cultures, our jobs, our clothing, or our makeup. They know us as no one else does, in our private joys, angry rages, deepest despair, in sickness and in health. All the while, their calm steady presence gives us an unwavering love like few others on Earth. Our animal companions see through us to the very soul of our soul, encouraging the unfolding of a sacred trust. If there is such a thing as a soul mate, then surely this is it.

—Sharon Callahan, animal communicator

🐾 AGE 🐾

Nonhuman animals generally have a more accepting attitude about aging, dying, and death than do most humans in our Western society. Most of the animals I've met are not concerned about how old they are. Without hesitation, they give their age as how young they feel or their actual body age. Most just naturally go about enjoying their life until it's time to leave the Earth. However, if humans have communicated negative feelings about aging, the animals around them may feel threatened about being a certain age.

Boogie, a cat who was doing well and had no physical problems at eighteen years old, became quite ill. It turned out that several people had made a big deal about how old she was. They exclaimed how amazing it was that she was still alive. When I counseled Boogie through the upsetting feeling that she was supposed to be dead, she felt relieved and started to recover. I advised her human companion not to mention Boogie's age in the future. Boogie lived to be twenty-two years old.

🐾 HUMAN EMOTION 🐾

Human emotional attachment can make animal companions cling to a torturous existence when they would normally prepare themselves for their transitions peacefully. Dying in a situation surrounded by frantic emotion or sudden unwanted change can be confusing and traumatic for animals, making their transition into the spiritual realm more difficult. Animals may also choose to leave when they are alone, so they can go in peace without causing suffering to their human companions.

A Scottish terrier named Angus was getting old and knew his body was dying. His human companion called me when Angus became ill. The dog relayed to me that he didn't want a big fuss made over him when it was his time to go. Angus was taken to the vet with a high fever, 105 degrees. The veterinarian did what he could with antibiotics, but when the fever failed to subside, he said he could do no more. Angus raised his head when his human companion called me. Angus was quite definite in his wishes. He didn't want a protracted death because it would be too emotionally painful for his human companion and himself. Angus wanted his companion to know how much he loved her and that he would stay around after his death to guide her until it was his time to move on. She wanted to know if Angus should be put to sleep. Angus told me he would be going soon and didn't mind if it was with assistance from the vet.

Tuning into what your animal friend wants to communicate requires being quiet and calming your own thoughts, emotions, and distractions as much as possible. We are all close to our animal companions and are able to feel what they feel, even if no one has taught us how. Obviously, when we are emotionally distraught over an animal's death, it can be difficult to be open and listen. Yet, most people confirm that they understand the communications I receive from their animal friends, at least partially. It rings true to them as something they innately understand from knowing their animal friends and having received the animal's telepathic communication before, whether consciously or not. Opening up to animal communication and acknowledging it helps us to develop it further. In matters of life and death, being able to engage in two-way communication with our animal friends is of supreme value.

Elizabeth Severino, animal communicator, tells how Sleepy, a 21-year-old beagle, spared his human companion the agony of witnessing his death:

Sleepy had been with his human, Fred, throughout his entire life. Sleepy was mostly an outside dog. Fred had constructed a wonderful dog house for him, complete with insulation and a shingled roof. Sleepy was quite happy.

Sleepy knew, however, that when he crossed over it would be extremely difficult for Fred, so when Fred left for an extended business trip, Sleepy dug out of the backyard, a behavior he hadn't shown in many years. He was taken into a household and hidden by a neighborhood boy, who was housebound and suffering from an unusual infectious disease.

The boy's mother eventually realized Sleepy was hidden in her son's room and took appropriate action, but it was too late. Sleepy's internal organs were deteriorating, and he needed to be euthanized by the attending veterinarian.

When I contacted Sleepy's essence after Fred returned, Sleepy was quite clear. He had orchestrated the entire event to save Fred the suffering of watching him die, which Sleepy felt would be too great for Fred to bear.

You may have had an animal friend die when you were not around. It doesn't mean you did anything wrong. Animals need to focus on their impending departure. It takes all their remaining energy to let go of their physical form and their energetic connections to life. They often spend increasing amounts of time in the spiritual dimension long before they finally leave their body. Through this process, they become less connected to Earth. As they are dying, animals usually want peace and a sense of calmness in the people around them so they can detach their energies and lift out of the body without trauma to themselves and their human companions, if possible. Other animal family members often model the quiet vigilance and reverence for the animal who is departing.

🐾 LENGTH OF THE JOURNEY 🐾

Sometimes animals travel a long journey to death over months or even years, leaving gradually with their physical senses becoming duller. They may increasingly spend more time out of their bodies in the spiritual realm. Their connection with the Earth and their physical body becomes more tenuous. They may become weak and disoriented, and display different behavior than their formerly vital selves. I have seen some animals get very quiet, while some cats and dogs vocalize much more. They may communicate that their purpose for this life is completed or they are tired. They may realize their body is failing and want to let go. Sometimes animals may repeat a rollercoaster ride of plunging toward death and then making miraculous recoveries.

People often want to know when an animal will die or whether they are suffering and need help from the veterinarian to depart. They want to do what is best for the animal. When you can communicate with animals and find out what's happening with them—which can change from moment to moment—it helps make the process much easier for all involved. You won't necessarily be able to predict the exact time of death, but you will be able to find out about the changing feelings and condition of your animal friend.

Sometimes animals have a strong sense of knowing when they will depart, and they communicate it clearly. My Afghan hound, Rana, who was showing signs of slowing down, helped prepare me by telling me she would die in two weeks. She told me she would not need veterinary assistance but would die on her own. She proceeded to get weaker, each day losing a bit more of her ability to stand and go outside to relieve herself, until finally she couldn't get up at all. I gently tended to her needs as I watched her life force ebb. During her last three days, she did not want to eat, and she would not drink on her last day in this world. Exactly two weeks from when she told me she would depart, she left her body, which convulsed as she detached from it. This was hard to watch. It was 4 AM, and I decided to call the vet for assistance as soon as his office opened. However, Rana left soon after the convulsions began, with peace and dignity as she had chosen.

A woman called animal communicator Barbara Janelle to ask her whether she should have surgery done on her twelve-year-old dog to remove a non-malignant growth on his neck. Barbara's response was: "I felt the dog was too old for surgery, but when I asked the dog, he said, 'I will live one year without the surgery. With the surgery, I will live one year in much greater comfort.'"

I relayed this information to my client, who decided to have the surgery done. The dog lived comfortably for one more year.

Not all animals are this clear about when it's their time to leave, even though they are apparently dying. Animals often make dramatic recoveries after they receive healing bodywork and counseling for emotional upsets and traumas related to the illness or injury.

🐾 HUMAN ATTITUDES AND TREATMENT 🐾

Domesticated and captive wild animals may become confused or fear what will happen to them in human environments. Some pick up human fears about death. Animal companions sometimes dread dying because of the grief it causes and the obligation they feel to live as long as possible for the sake of their human companions. Many domesticated animals consciously incarnate to be with specific people to support, love, and guide them. They often become like their human companions in their mannerisms, ways of thinking, and emotional states. No matter the species, social creatures tend to become more like each other, either unconsciously or from a desire to be closer and more compatible with their family or mates.

Animal companions are not simply extensions of the humans they live with, mimicking what they perceive from humans. They also have their own minds and their own ideas about who they are and why they're here. They are able to make and act on their own decisions, within the limits of their domestic situation. Animals, like other family members, can echo the illnesses and emotional states of their human companions. They may be consciously or unconsciously attempting to help or heal humans, or they are simply adopting the energy patterns that surround and bombard them because they are more or less dependent on people.

Treating an animal with respect as a fellow being enhances their sense of security, boosts their confidence, and adds to their enjoyment of life. With a caring, respectful attitude from humans, even insecure or abused animals can become more of their natural, whole selves.

How does this apply to dying? Animals who have become too dependent on humans may approach death in an unnatural way. They may worry about hurting their human families when they die. Instead of leaving in a dignified and peaceful manner, with the understanding and approval of their human companions, they may feel they have to undergo every possible treatment and hang on despite great suffering and debilitation. In contrast, other animals know they absolutely do not want continued surgeries or other therapies, and they may withdraw emotionally or physically if humans do not listen to and honor their wishes.

If you are confused about what is going on with your animal friend, stop what you are doing. Sit quietly and feel your feet on the ground, connected to the Earth. Allow yourself time to breathe deeply until your emotions and worries about your animal friend subside.

Keep focusing on your breathing and let go of mental and emotional distractions, until you can be more focused, clear, and present with your animal friend.

Feel your connection to your animal friend through your feet on the ground. Allow yourself to find an open space in your mind and heart to receive what is going on with the animal besides your own worries about them. You may be able to receive the animal's wishes and feelings. Allow yourself to honor and feel your own emotions and responses, too. You will be better able to decide the best course of action after receiving and honoring both your own and the animal's feelings.

🐾 HANDLING ANIMAL DEATH 🐾

There is no prescription for how to die. Each case is individual. Sometimes transitions that seem the most agonizing have a deeper purpose behind them, and the beings concerned grow in profound ways during the process. Let me give some examples of the different ways my clients have handled the deaths of their animals, including illness and death from the viewpoint of the animals. Except in the case of my own animal family, or when granted permission, fictitious names have been used to honor the privacy of those involved.

Joan called me about her fourteen-year-old collie, Frieda, who had arthritis. She felt the dog was in severe pain and should be put to sleep. Frieda, however, made it clear to me that although she was stiff and had a hard time getting around, she wasn't suffering intolerable pain and didn't want to go just yet. She felt her life was not complete; she needed a few more months with her human family. The pain did not bother her to the extent Joan thought it did. Frieda said that when she felt her time had come, she would let Joan know by looking at her and saying goodbye. In the meantime, I recommended acupuncture treatments to make the dog more comfortable.

Months later, Frieda had reached the point where she could no longer move by herself. She looked at Joan, who then knew it was time for the vet to assist Frieda's departure from the body. Everyone was prepared, and Frieda made a peaceful transition from the physical plane.

Like Joan, you can also stay in touch with your animal friends about the timing of death. Being able to experience the rightness of knowing when they are ready to go will help you be ready, too.

Mary had two dogs of a sporting breed, father and daughter, named Joey and Lily. Joey developed symptoms of back pain and neurological disorders, causing him to scream in pain and attack his rear end, particularly on walks. Standard veterinary treatment, acupuncture, herbs, and homeopathic remedies, plus counseling and spiritual healing alleviated his symptoms somewhat. However, it was a rollercoaster ride until his death, which was protracted and wrought with emotional pain for Mary.

A year or so after Joey's death, Lily began to demonstrate similar symptoms. After several trips to the vet didn't help, Mary called me to find out what was going on and what could be done. Lily was not only biting herself, but she had also attacked and severely hurt the cat companion she had been friendly with previously. Mary was in great distress about what to do.

I had a hard time tuning into Lily because the pain she suffered was so severe. I had to be frank with Mary about what Lily communicated, stating it in the kindest way possible, but Mary had a hard time accepting it. I recommended that she take Lily to see the vet again to help relieve the dog's pain.

Mary had a hard time facing euthanasia for her animals, even when it was obvious their suffering was severe and their quality of life was poor. I tried to guide her towards accepting death as a part of life, and I reassured her that it would be okay to send Lily on to her next phase of existence if her pain could not be alleviated. I cautioned Mary that not only would Lily hurt the cat again, but she might also attack humans. Mary kept asking me if I was sure Lily was in great pain. After all, she reasoned, Lily still wagged her tail and cuddled up to her between bouts of screaming.

Lily was so distraught that she didn't know what she wanted or what she was doing. She did not want to suffer. Death was not frightening to her, in itself, but she watched Mary for what to do and feel. I don't know what happened to Lily. Mary wrote me a note saying she should never have called me. It was sad to see so much pain and suffering result from Mary's fear of death and her inability to face what was going on with her dog.

Karen had an aging cat named Paprika, who was slowly dying of kidney failure. While Karen had many animal companions of various kinds, she was particularly close to Paprika and couldn't bear the thought of her dying. With the help of the vet and then Karen giving Paprika subcutaneous fluids, Paprika managed to hang on for months, sometimes feeling fairly energetic and sometimes feeling exhausted but not in severe pain.

Karen kept in touch with me about how Paprika was doing physically, emotionally, and spiritually. Paprika was willing to go through the veterinary care needed to keep her going, and she wanted to be close to Karen throughout the dying process.

During the months of caring for Paprika and deepening their communication, Karen became more and more able to release her cat. She realized that death didn't need to be a horrible, devastating process. Paprika grew in love and patience, and she taught Karen about death and her own nature as a spiritual being. By the time Paprika peacefully left her body, both she and Karen were ready. They had gained a tremendous amount from the dying process. Karen was aware of Paprika's spiritual presence after her death, and the communion they felt eased the physical loss.

You can help yourself and your animal friends by focusing on their and your own spiritual nature and connection, shifting into a loving celebration of your life together and your connection beyond the physical form.

Suzanne had gone through the painful process of trying to keep her Doberman, Trader, alive, even though he had heart and kidney problems. In desperation, she had tried a myriad of drugs and treatments, causing Trader severe emotional and physical trials. They echoed each other's fear of loss, and both suffered extremely during the dying process.

Fortunately, Suzanne learned from the gruesome death of Trader. When her cat, Peanut, developed cancer, she decided she would not make decisions for him or try to make him stay. She told him he was free to leave whenever and in whatever manner he chose. She offered him gentle healing treatments if he wanted them. Peanut was active and happy over a year later without extreme medical treatment.

Suzanne now blesses her animal friends for the gift of coming into her life and acknowledges that they are also free to go. What a difference this kind of attitude can make to the quality of our relationships with animals.

🐾 READINESS 🐾

So much of how the dying process evolves for those involved depends upon a being's readiness to leave this world. Animals appreciate being listened to and honored during their illness or dying process, when their energy ebbs and flows. It comforts them and can make it easier for them to continue living or to die peacefully.

Joanna Seere tells of her experience with Phyo, a remarkable cat who demonstrated the art of surrender, acceptance, and grace as he allowed Joanna to be by his side on his final journey:

Phyo (pronounced "Fee-oh") came to me through his person Mandy, a sensitive and caring woman who works as a therapist and lives with her husband, two-year-old son, and Roo, Phyo's brother. Phyo and Roo were dumped and rescued from the trash cans of New York City twelve years before. In their life with Mandy, they blossomed into loving family members, yet always retained some aspects of their early trauma.

When Mandy called me, Phyo had been diagnosed with a highly aggressive squamous cell carcinoma in the nasal cavity. The prognosis was extremely poor.

Mandy was concerned with honoring Phyo and his wishes as well as honoring her own feelings and choices. It became clear in our communications with Phyo that he was not ready to die. Even more than that, he was extremely specific about not wanting any aggressive treatment in which he would be held or feel forced. Mandy was determined to do right by Phyo for whatever time he had and in whatever way he asked. She did not want him to suffer and she wanted to be sure that if he needed assistance in leaving his body, she would know.

What became clear to me as we started our sessions was the process of surrender that was unfolding in Phyo as he released the residual trauma of his kittenhood and the places where he had not been fully free in his life. Mandy began reporting to me that Phyo seemed happier than he had ever been in his life. Something had lifted, and he was more balanced and joyful. The more I worked with him, the more ecstatic he became and the more golden his energy appeared psychically to me. He was radiant, almost translucent.

Mandy also saw a beautiful golden glow surrounding Phyo. He became more affectionate and asked for deeper physical contact with Mandy. He was losing weight and Mandy noticed the greater demands of the tumor as it began pressing into his eye socket and distorting his appearance. Yet Phyo was happy, deeply affectionate, and at peace.

Living with a type of cancer that is known to be fast moving, highly disfiguring, and extraordinarily painful, Phyo experienced no pain, only differences in how he felt in his body. He seemed to come into a state of grace, forgiving the past, accepting his condition, and living in the exquisite now. His presence reminded me of pictures I've seen of the Buddha when he achieved Samadhi—golden, glowing, and joyful in acceptance and aliveness.

Mandy surrendered along with Phyo, allowing the moment-to-moment process to simply be. Phyo lived beyond the time predicted in his prognosis.

One day Mandy noticed that Phyo hadn't eaten. He went to his favorite napping spot behind the stereo console and didn't some out. Mandy called me, wondering what to do, and asked if he was alive or dead. When I connected with Phyo, he was so deeply alive in his spiritual essence that he wasn't sure if he was in his body or not. I was able to feel that he was gone from his body. Yet the move from the physical to the spiritual was so gentle, he had barely noticed. He had been walking in the two worlds so completely that crossing over was as simple as exhaling.

Mandy and I cried and rejoiced. How remarkably Phyo had demonstrated to us the process of living, letting go, and dying in grace through complete surrender into the presence of the Divine.

Since his passage, Phyo has been assisting his brother Roo in adjusting to his new life as the top cat. He has been witnessed as a bright and gentle presence, a guiding force in the lives of Roo, Mandy, and her children.

Domesticated animals can also be attached to their bodies, their lives, and their human companions and not want to leave, even when their bodies are in severe pain and no longer able to function. Loving understanding, use of flower essences or homeopathic remedies that help balance emotions and attachments, and spiritual healing can all ease the transition of an animal who doesn't want to let go, even when it's clearly insufferable to stay.

I experienced this with my Afghan, Pasha, who struggled to live and tenaciously hung on when death was imminent. We used flower essences, healing energy, and prayer to help Pasha come to peace. When the vet administered the final injection, we all experienced great relief. Pasha was grateful, and his spirit flew free and clear.

🐾 SUDDEN DEATH 🐾

Animals whose death is sudden and happens without their conscious choice may feel confused and not even know they are "dead." A German shepherd who was hit by a car and her body catapulted next to a fence, kept telling me she was behind a fence and couldn't find her way home. Communication and counseling enabled her to release the trauma of her accident. She was then able to make her way with joy as a spirit and let go of the idea and images of being a dog behind a fence, trying to get back to her human companion.

Barbara Janelle talks about a client who suddenly decided to have her elderly horse put down:

> The horse was not told about what was going to happen, nor was Ellen, the farm owner, until the vet arrived and told her what he was there to do. The vet euthanized Joe in front of the barn near the basketball hoop.
>
> For three days, Ellen's dog, Ruskie, went to the area in front of the barn, looked up at the basketball hoop, and barked. Joe was hanging around up there, quite puzzled about the whole situation. I told the former horse that he was out of his body now and could leave with our gratitude for all the joy he had brought to our lives. Ruskie stopped barking immediately and never barked at the hoop again.

I usually check with animals who have been killed on the road to see if they have gone on successfully or whether they are still hanging around the body, confused and possibly needing help to reorient. Just acknowledging the sudden trauma of their departure usually sends them happily on their way. Some do not tarry in the spiritual realm but, like going through a revolving door, go right on to fulfill their purpose by being reborn in a similar form. You can practice helping out in this way, too.

Animals who experience traumatic or confusing deaths usually recover their spiritual balance quickly without the help of human communication and counseling. They have an awareness of death as a part of life and themselves as spirit. Swift, expected death, such as that between wild predator and prey, is accepted and does not create residual confusion. Animals, wild or domestic, who make conscious choices to live and die in a certain way, and feel their purpose has been fulfilled, move on quite happily. With domesticated animals, it often helps when humans understand and honor the choices the animals have made.

🐾 NATURAL DEPARTURE 🐾

Ideally, we would like animals to be born and die peacefully, surrounded by love. The experience of moving from life to life for most beings on Earth, throughout history, includes the gamut of traumatic deaths, from accidents, murder, war, slaughter, abuse, torture, and neglect. It's a precious gift to honor a being of any species in their birth, life, and death, and help change the tide of suffering to peace, tranquility, and loving care for all.

Physical bodies are programmed to survive, and when they determinedly keep pumping blood and breath, it can be difficult for the spirit to depart, despite its intentions. Sometimes holding animal companions and giving them energy, or constantly ministering to their bodies, can make it more painful or impossible for them to leave. Human emotions and thoughts can also be distracting. Each case is different. Some animals want you to be there to comfort and hold them as they go. It's also common for animals, including humans, to die when everyone leaves them alone. They often need that quiet space in order to focus on the spiritual realm and make a peaceful transition.

It's natural to slow down with an animal as they slow down during their passage towards death. Try to create as much comfort as possible for all involved in the sometimes painful, emotional process. Give yourself time to feel the deep feelings and growth that are evoked as your heart breaks and opens during this sacred passage. It's important to honor your own emotions, to clear yourself emotionally, and to honor the animal's emotions and desires about dying.

My Afghan hound, Buddha Boy, left his body in November 2005. A few days before he died, he asked me to lie down next to him and hold him full length for the last time. After that he wanted me to touch him only minimally. Throughout his last few days, he wanted silence, no music or distractions, and just to know that I was around. I honored the tenderness of this time, filling vases with flowers from the garden and surrounding Buddha's space with them. I lit candles and created a special altar with sacred objects. Belinda, our female dog companion, respectfully lay a few feet from Buddha to keep vigil for periods of time.

I have been blessed to have many animal companions of different species grace my life. Most of them have departed without veterinary assistance. When the spirit separates from the body and the body organ systems are shutting down, the animal may whimper or moan. This may concern us, but it's often part of the process of detachment. There may be convulsions and evacuation of body wastes at or near the final break of spirit from body.

Buddha Boy had specifically requested to go on his own without veterinary intervention. On his last day, he breathed heavily and whimpered on and off. He could not get up and did not want me to assist him in going outside to relieve himself, which he had previously been able to do alone. I had already assured him, and myself, that it was okay to let go. Animals sometimes hang on and suffer needlessly without this "permission" from their human companions.

As I kept in touch with Buddha during the final steps of his life journey, I could feel at times that he was reluctant to let go, but he realized there was no turning back. His body was becoming a burden to him. On the last day, I felt that if his suffering escalated I might have to call the vet, but Buddha Boy assured me he could manage the breakdown of his organs and the level of pain he experienced as he moved into death. He told me I could call the vet if he had not left by the following day.

I asked the angels, ancestor spirits, the Great Mother, the Divine within and around us all, and all of our guides and animal family who had gone before to assist Buddha in a gentle departure. We had already done a life review during the last few weeks, forgiven mis-understandings, and celebrated our experiences together. I felt that during this phase of dying, Buddha was completing the final part of his life mission.

I stayed with him during his final hours until I got too tired, and then I rested on my bed near him. I fell asleep and when I awoke a few hours later, he had left his body. His face looked peaceful. At first, I felt sorry I had not been awake with him in the moment of his departure. Buddha Boy's spirit immediately assured me that it was fine that I was not there during his final throes. Only he could take that part of the journey, and he was glad to have spared me the physical convulsion that was needed to depart. When I felt his expanded presence, my heart filled with the deepest love.

Soon after he took his last breath, he experienced his true state of being. He had many realizations about the different phases of his work with me during his life and why our journey together had to be the way it was. It was illuminating and poignantly sacred for both of us. He kept in constant communion with me, and I felt bathed in a new level of love from him and all life. Inspired to near wordlessness, I am still unable to fully express all that happened during this passage. Buddha Boy had lived with me and helped me with my work for over twelve years, and I was grateful.

It felt right to leave his body in state that day. I cleaned up his bodily wastes as best I could, surrounded him with flowers, and continued to burn candles in his honor. I had already begun digging his grave next to the grave of his former Afghan companion, Reya, who had died three years before. Late that day, the time felt right to take his body to the grave site. I usually place the bodies of my animal friends in the grave on top of a piece of my clothing and/or their favorite blanket. I put the blanket Buddha had used to keep warm during his final weeks into the grave, along with a favorite old sweatshirt of mine. I put his body on top of them and surrounded and covered his body with flowers, crystals, and favorite stones. I did not feel it was time to return his body to the Earth completely, so I covered the grave with a sheet for the night and completed the burial ceremony in the morning, adding more flowers and his favorite treats before I covered his body with soil and mounded the grave.

During the hallowed time right after Buddha's death, past animal family members—most of whose bodies are buried on the land we all shared, called the "Floating Island of Peace"—came for a reunion visit. Wherever I walked in the garden, and as I sat by Buddha's grave, I would meet these wonderful friends in spirit, who had been cats, dogs, rabbits, birds, chickens, lizards, rats, llama, and guinea pigs. Together, we celebrated the completion of a whole phase of life together and the start of something new.

I felt Buddha Boy's presence intensely, so rich and deep with love, for the first week after he died. He wanted me to be happy and showered blessings upon my life to help me in the future. He contacted many people who had known him and shared his radiant expansiveness with them. I continued to feel a deepening of our connection and love, which grew greater with time.

🐾 DISPOSITION OF THE BODY 🐾

Most of the animals I have communicated with are not attached to their former bodies after death and don't concern themselves about the disposition of their bodies. However, some ask that their bodies be buried in a certain place or in a certain way. Some ask for their bodies to be cremated and the ashes spread in a particular place. Most see and enjoy the love that people express during ceremonies held in their honor. It helps create a feeling of completion for all concerned so that both humans and nonhumans can move on in the physical or spiritual realm. A client wrote to me regarding her Great Dane's death:

Thank you so much for helping me during our phone consultation. About three weeks later, I woke up knowing without any doubt that it was time to help him leave. I felt that he and I had talked on the astral plane, so I made the vet appointment and told him about it. He understood and was scared that night, but for his last three days he was like his old self and did all the things he did before getting so sick. It was such a special gift for both of us. He went to sleep peacefully and was ecstatic to be out of his old body. He is with me often. We buried his bones in the deep of a redwood grove and planted a redwood seedling over them.

I miss him greatly, but he is happy, so I am not as grief-stricken as I thought I'd be.

Beings who have gone on generally feel free without their physical form. They are more concerned with how their families are doing emotionally than with what happens to their old bodies. They may hang around or check in for a time to ensure that their loved ones are okay, sending love and blessings, or directing a new animal companion to the family. Applying your animal communication skills at this time can be rewarding and profound. You can blessedly continue to feel the connection and your animal friend's spiritual presence in your life.

Some animals reincarnate when it's time for them to do so. More on that subject later....

3

Letting Go and Euthanasia

The beauty of sharing a life with an animal comes with the guaranteed opportunity to share the beauty of the death experience, no matter what form it takes. With the ending of the physical relationship with your animal companion, you have the opportunity to open, widen, and deepen your telepathic skills in the spiritual arena, to communicate with them on another level, enriching your shared bond even further.

—Joan Fox, animal communicator

🐾 HOW YOU WILL KNOW 🐾

*I*t's vital to know and be sensitive to what animals feel about their own life and death process. If they are fighting to live, want to get well, and are willing to undergo potentially helpful treatments, then that's the way to support them. Sometimes, animals who can't even move without human assistance want to keep living and be of service to their human companions. The inspiration, love, and growth that animals and humans derive from each other cannot be measured.

It may be hard to know when to end treatment and let go. Your animal companions may not know either. They often wish to do what will make you feel better, even if it means continuing with painful or useless treatment. With the help of your veterinarian's diagnosis, your own intuition, and direct communication with your animal friends about their feelings and wishes, the transition to death can be made easier. Although the loss of the animal's physical presence is saddening, and we need to honor our grief and let our feelings flow, the connection with the animal as spirit helps to put the whole process into perspective.

Even if you understand animals easily, it can be difficult to know if and when it's okay to assist them in their dying process using euthanasia. Your desire to have the animal live or your worry about their death may block clear communication.

Even if an animal companion asks to go in their own way and time, the situation may change. They might need help in leaving the body if they are suffering excessively. Ask them to let you know. Being so close to them, you can feel their wishes and interpret their signs. When you can allow yourself to breathe, connect to the Earth, and open your heart to what is truly best for all concerned, you will know what to do.

When they feel their bodies deteriorating, some animals say: "Let me go now. Help me along before I lose my dignity." Sitting quietly with your animal friends, listening as best you can, making peace with them, going over the life you've had together, and being willing to let them go are the best things to do when it's obvious that life can no longer be sustained. Many animals can then go quietly and happily. Even with the sadness of losing their physical presence, it's possible to experience their joy in being a free spirit when the body dies. You can learn to maintain a spiritual connection and communication with your departed friends, which also helps to put the whole process in perspective. Elizabeth Severino tells about Bodie, a 14-year-old dog who clearly knew what he wanted:

Bodie was losing the ability to function. During our consultation he told us the integrity of his internal organs was failing, and he was losing mobility in his rear leg. He was quite clear that he would give several signs to his human companion: he would lose his appetite; he would experience loss of urinary and bowel control; he would emit a moaning sound, which would steadily increase; and his leg would fail completely. It would be clear at that time, he told us, that his "bad" days would be outnumbering his "good" days. He further advised us that he wanted all "pushing and prodding" to stop. He anticipated that the playing out of the body's deterioration to the point of wanting assistance in leaving would take three to four weeks. Later, his human companion advised me that three weeks to the day, all of the signs became evident.

It's natural to seek the best treatment you can to help restore an animal's health. If you are also willing to view death as a natural, profound, and even beautiful part of life, it becomes easier for the animal to relax and either get well or leave peacefully. Accept your emotions as they come, but don't put the burden on your animal friends to handle your feelings by requiring them to hang on to life. Listen to them and keep in touch with their spiritual nature. Understand their viewpoints, and let death, like life, be a growing process.

🐾 LESSONS IN LETTING GO 🐾

Learning to let go and surrender to the flow of life and death is an ongoing process that we experience in different ways during our time on Earth.

One woman had to release her lost dog as dead before she could allow the dog to come back into her life alive. Animal communicator Karen Anderson tells how she attempted to help the woman find her dog, Shadow, who had run away (Exerpt from the book *Hear All Creatures!*):

I connected telepathically with the dog, Shadow, who told me she was still alive, just upset and disoriented. She said she had gone south of her home, and even had an opportunity to go to other people, but she was too scared to approach them. Shadow relayed an image of herself hunkered down near an old truck close to a fence and a field.

The woman was on an emotional rollercoaster. She posted signs everywhere for Shadow and went door to door in the farming region, talking to anyone who would listen. She called me frequently over the next week to see if I had received any more clues from Shadow. She drove the back roads day after day, calling for Shadow. No one had seen her dog.

The woman contacted a psychic and asked whether Shadow was still alive. The psychic told her, "No, the dog died several days ago." The psychic said the "Shadow" I was talking to was the spirit of Shadow, now feeling younger, happier, and loving life on the other side. The woman called me in tears, saying she now knew that Shadow was dead. She thanked me and said she was going to say good-bye to [Shadow] with a quiet ceremony at home. Emotionally spent, she resigned herself to the fact that her dog was dead.

A few days later, Shadow contacted me and told me that her human companion needed to learn how to let go. This was one of the lessons Shadow was here to teach her. Once she let go, Shadow would return. Shadow acknowledged that this lesson would be difficult and create intense emotional trauma, but it was necessary for the woman's spiritual growth. Shadow again told me that she was still alive, just cold and hungry (it was November).

I felt compelled to deliver Shadow's messages, even though the woman had told me her dog was dead. The woman said she had a ceremony the night before to say her final good-byes to her beloved Shadow. She thanked me again and said she felt better now that she had closure.

Several days later, I received an e-mail from her that said: "Shadow is alive and home!" A man saw one of the woman's flyers and remembered he had seen Shadow hunkered down in some tall grass near a radio-controlled air strip about five miles south of her home. Shadow was shivering and extremely thin, but the vet said she was okay.

The universe had played out the events exactly as they needed to happen. Without the psychic telling the woman Shadow was dead, she might not have learned to fully let go.

Joan Fox discovered during the dying process of her dog, Bo, that it was her own pain that was unmanageable, not the dog's pain. She explained,

"Bo was mirroring to me that there were places within me that needed healing. It was my pain that needed to be 'put down,' not Bo."

Sometimes animals develop life-threatening diseases and are near death, but then they make a surprising recovery. In other cases, an animal's physical condition may be deteriorating badly, and they hold on in a debilitated state. Often, this is because their human guardians are not ready to let them go. The extra time to be with their animal friends is enough for everyone to honor the life they had together and come to terms with the release of death.

There may be profound lessons to be learned during the time before an animal departs. When animals have the opportunity to express their feelings—and humans have the opportunity to accept and face their own feelings of love, grief, pain, helplessness, and all the pleasure they have had in living with their departing animal friend— everyone can more easily come to release and peaceful closure.

It helps to look at what the animal has taught and given us before we can let go of the emotions that inhibit us from shifting into a heartfelt, open, relief-filled feeling of gratitude. This helps us let go and allows our animal friends to relax into dying with peace and love. Animal communicators, counselors, friends, animal guides, our animal companions themselves, and our own intuitive communication ability may all have a part in assisting our process of release.

🐾 LEAVING IN THEIR OWN TIME 🐾

Animals often give a clear indication they want to die or continue to live if you observe them with an open heart and mind, or just directly ask them.

Barbara Janelle tells of a thirty-year-old mare named Blue, who went down in her stall one evening. The horse's guardian and veterinarian came. The mare looked to be at death's door. The woman knelt down beside Blue and said, "Now, Blue, I need a clear signal. Do you want to die now?" Blue opened her eyes, looked at her guardian, and got to her feet. She lived for several more years.

Marta Guzmán learned a lot about surrendering to love from a cat she didn't like.

I had an orange tabby cat named Petey, whom I adored. When Petey was five months old, I adopted Angela, a black and white short-haired cat. Petey loved Angela, but I felt at odds with her and kept her at a distance.

Years later, Angela was diagnosed with renal failure. I was surprised at my grief-stricken reaction to the news. I administered subcutaneous fluids for thirteen months, and Angela fared well with the treatment. Then her condition deteriorated severely. I called the vet to have her put down, but I canceled the appointment when Angela suddenly improved enormously.

I realized that Angela and I were no longer fighting each other, and I could finally open my heart and listen to what she wanted, which was to go in her own time. We had a loving three weeks together, during which she grew weaker each day. One day when I returned from a meeting, I found her at rest [near] her bed. We had made peace at the end. I realized that Angela had taught me so much about giving in to love, and I was grateful.

Doris had been advised by her friends and the vet to put her cat, Poppy, to sleep. Poppy could not function without Doris feeding her by hand and manually helping her eliminate bodily wastes. When I talked to Poppy, she told me she wanted to go in her own way and not be euthanized. She felt okay about Doris's ministrations because Doris did not consider it a burden and treated her with dignity.

Poppy left her body peacefully one day while Doris was away. She told us afterwards that she didn't want Doris to worry about her, so Poppy chose to die when Doris wasn't home. Poppy described meeting other beings who had died before her, including Doris's relatives and other animal companions, and a whole group of beings who were Poppy's friends. Doris told me how her mother, who was long dead, had communicated in a dream that she would be there for Poppy.

These spiritual connections and revelations added a sacred perspective and much peace for Doris. You may find that similar experiences lighten your path when your animal dies, even if you have no previous belief or experience in spiritual phenomena. Being open to these possibilities can add to feeling peaceful and connected to others.

Sherri's old horse, Mamba, was dying of cancer despite surgeries and herbal and homeopathic treatments. It was becoming hard for her to eat or move. Sherri and Mamba had made their peace, and both agreed it was the right time for the vet to come and assist her departure.

Mamba was popular with the people at the stables and asked to say good-bye. Sherri arranged for Mamba's friends to come to a going away party for her, and she wanted to know if Mamba desired anything special for the party. In her communication with me, Mamba pictured herself wearing a party hat and eating carrot cake. Sherri laughed, because Mamba had worn a hat and eaten carrot cake at previous birthday parties.

It was a wonderful party, with tears and warmth and joy shared for Mamba's good life. The next day, when the vet came, Mamba was ready and lay down to accept the injection. She left with peace and dignity, in the style she had lived. Sherri felt relieved and happy for her horse, instead of guilty and burdened.

Neil Jarrell had a special love for his cat, Raku. When Raku started losing her sense of balance, the veterinarian diagnosed the cat's illness as terminal and offered to put her down, which was devastating for Neil. He tells what happened.

I consulted animal communicator Val Heart, who assured me that Raku said it was not yet her time. The spring season was so rich, and she wanted to stay outside as long as she could. Raku didn't understand my hectic behavior and invited me to experience some "power spots" she loved to position herself over in the backyard.

I spent time with Raku lying in the grass, trying to slow my urges to jump up and get back to work or get away from the bugs, or solve a mental problem. Raku was trying to teach me to just "be."

During my emotional ordeal, I checked with Val a few times—one time about putting Raku to sleep. Raku's response was to thank me for my concern, but she didn't want to be put to sleep. She wanted the natural experience of this life transition. She said if the pain became too great, she would give a sign. Raku also told me, through Val, that she loved me very much, she was going on to a better place, and that the spirit continues. One afternoon, while out of my sight, Raku slipped away. I realized how much I had learned from my teacher, Raku, and how much humanity could learn if we would just listen to other species.

Catherine's dachshund, Julia, was severely injured with severed spinal discs, but she didn't want to die. She persisted with high spirits, though it took one year for her to walk again. Twice previously when she had slipped discs, the vet had advised euthanasia, but that was not Julia's way.

Loving and affectionate, Julia pictured to me life after life in many forms, including human, where she had served others despite physical suffering, always going beyond it. The lessons she wanted to share by example were that suffering is a way of thinking and that physical pain doesn't have to stop a being from serving and loving. What a joy to meet such a humble, beautiful, advanced being.

You may not be able to receive the full depth of communication if you are just beginning to practice animal communication. However, knowing that your animal friends have profound wisdom to share opens you to the possibility of discovering more of what they have to give.

Joan Fox tells this beautiful story of her animal friend orchestrating his departure and the amazing responses of the other animals:

Bo and Annie, our eleven-year-old littermate Lhasa-poos, were our constant companions. As family members, they were included in hikes and on camping trips. Annie continued to be forever spunky, but Bo started to slow down considerably. A vet check confirmed my telepathic scan. Bo had multiple tumors and was suffering from congestive heart failure. With great sadness, I asked Bo how I could make him more comfortable. Was he in pain? Did he want surgery or need medication? And the dreaded question: Did he want to be eased out of his misery? I told him we would do whatever he asked.

Bo, always a "man" of few words, responded gruffly, "I'm not going to the vet. I'll take care of it."

I continued to snuggle him on my lap every day, while retelling and reliving old memories and escapades. At that point, I could actually laugh about the time I came home from work to find that he and Annie, our two-year-old puppies, had literally unraveled an entire hallway of new carpet!

As his breathing became more and more labored, the agony of watching him gasp for breath gripped every cell of my body. When I revisited the old question, he always responded firmly, "I AM NOT going to the vet!"

A few weeks later, my former husband, Joe, and I were home from work on Friday [for] a holiday weekend. I looked at Bo and said, "Bo, I can't take watching you suffer anymore. You are going to have to help me out. My heart is breaking. I'm calling the vet and taking you in."

This time he didn't respond telepathically. He just walked over and licked my leg. I knew he had resigned himself to the inevitable. True to animal conduct, he had honored my wish with unconditional love. I called the vet at 9:00 AM, but because it was a holiday, she was out of town. I was informed that the doctor on call could not see Bo until 3:00 PM.

Standing in the doorway to the patio, I crumpled in sobs. Bo gathered his strength, licked my face, and then ambled outside and lay down under the glass patio table. The next few hours would be forever burned in my memory.

Bo was under the table, and I was seated in the doorway, when Fergie, our huge gray and white cat appeared. We had always thought she was mute. She had no fear of Bo and seemingly no previous interest in him. To her, he was just an annoyance she occasionally had to chase from my lap.

She stepped out of the open door, planted herself next to me, threw her head back, and yowled for thirty minutes without interruption. Hearing Fergie's voice for the first time, all five of our other animal companions quickly gathered. Each one knew Bo's hours were numbered, and Fergie was clearly delivering his eulogy. She performed royally, naming all of the things that she admired about Bo. She started with how amazed she was that in the 110-degree heat of Phoenix, Arizona, he would stumble out of the dog door and lie in the hottest part of the yard to soak up the sun. She said he was handsome and that she especially liked his coloring (the same as hers). Fergie voiced her appreciation to Bo for the respect he displayed, always leaving her to her own space and never chasing her. More than anything, she was happy he had never attempted to sit in my lap while I was at the computer. That space was reserved for her. When she had gleaned every last attribute of Bo's from her memory, she quietly curled up on my lap.

With this opening, Grandmother Squeaker, our orange tabby, leaped onto the patio table and peered at Bo through the heavy glass. Ever the "Being of Compassion," she thanked him for his years of loyal service to the family and surrounded him in loving light, blessing him on his journey.

Cheeto and Twiggy, our two feral kittens, inched through the doorway side by side, securely attached to each other at the hip, keeping a safe distance from Bo. He had terrorized them from the moment they were first brought into our family. Because of their highly sensitive feral wiring, they had been easy targets to intimidate. Cheeto and Twiggy sat silently for a couple of minutes, until Twiggy said, "If you can't say anything nice, don't say anything at all." They paid their respects with their presence and then darted back to the bedroom to hide.

Annie, Bo's littermate, sat speechless, gazing at him lovingly with huge, sad eyes.

We spent the next few hours telling Bo how much he was loved and treasured. Whenever I got up to move, Bo would struggle to his feet and follow me. Then a glance at the clock informed me it was time. As I combed my hair, I watched the reflection in the mirror and saw that Bo had turned around and left the bedroom. I knew it was the last time I would see him walk away. I dropped the brush and followed him. He lay on his side in the hallway. I called to Joe, and we lay down next to him on the floor. Annie lay with her head on her paws nearby. Bo gazed lovingly into our eyes, took three deep breaths, and passed. Annie immediately stood up and with resolve walked over, licked his face, turned and left. Without looking back she said, "Wow! Way to go, Bo!"

I now understand that Bo chose that particular day to leave because he knew we would be home. He let go of his tired, old body with his family around him. At the time, we were devastated by the loss of his physical presence, but we felt incredibly blessed that we had all been together to say good-bye. Bo's transition was his final gift to us.

🐾 WHEN THE BODY HANGS ON 🐾

Life on Earth can be seen as a huge recycling center. Species help each other live and die, and then live again in a continuous cycle of exchanging energy through our bodies. The same holds true on the spiritual level. We take on a form and live the life purpose we have chosen with varying degrees of consciousness, hopefully to the fullest. We let go and leave, spend time in other realms for varying intervals, and often return to the physical again in one form or another.

Some beings are ready for death, but their bodies won't let them go. The message "survive" is encoded in every cell. Bodies may not break down enough to let the residing spirit go peacefully. Sometimes, when the spirit has left the body or the veterinarian has delivered the fatal injection, even with the animal's permission, the body jerks and struggles to carry on cellular functioning. This can be disconcerting for people to watch, especially when they feel uncertain about assisting an animal in departing the Earth.

George, a senior cat, requested that he be given no more medication or forced feeding when he was too weak to eat. He wanted to be with his human companions for the last few days of his life. He asked me to assure them he was okay and that he had no pain as long as he didn't have to move much. He wanted to go on his own, which he felt would be soon.

His human companions spent much time with George, and both of them felt willing to let him go after telling him how much they loved and appreciated him. Four days later, he was much weaker but still alive. Everyone was amazed, but bodies sometimes work that way. His human companions asked him if the doctor could help ease his transition. George thought it over and said that as long as he didn't have to be moved, it would be okay. The veterinarian came to the house, and George had a peaceful departure.

Pamela called me when her aged horse, Chaco, was in extreme pain and scheduled for euthanasia. She wanted to make sure Chaco was okay about it. Chaco communicated that her body was no longer useful. She could not move because the pain in her feet was so intense, and she wanted assistance in departing. Pamela wrote to me:

> Chaco was put down within fifteen minutes of our call. This morning, as my dog and I were walking on the beach, I felt her presence. We were riding in the wind, once again—she snorting and with me petting her neck as her mane blew in my face. It was good.

🐾 MYSTICAL PREPARATION 🐾

We may also have precognitive dreams, visions, or mystical experiences that help us prepare for and move through the death of our animals. Animal communicator Cathy Malkin-Currea had an uncanny experience that prevented her dog's "accidental" death and helped her prepare for his later departure.

One afternoon, my keeshond KC (short for Kite Chaser) was eager to get across the street to play with his dog friend, Dakota. Out of the corner of my eye, I noticed a white car circling the neighborhood. The driver appeared to be looking at houses for sale.

As KC moved towards the road, a "movie" began to play out in my mind's eye: I saw the white car drive by and hit KC. Then I saw KC lying dead in the road, and I gave a blood curdling scream.

At that moment, KC was actually in the road. When I screamed, he turned instantly and ran back towards me. Only the tips of his hair had touched the car. Both relieved and upset, I felt that if I hadn't seen the imagined "movie" and screamed, KC would have died right before my eyes.

Later that afternoon, after returning from a neighbor's house, I found a large, dead dragonfly on my front doorstep in remarkably perfect condition. I felt the dragonfly was an omen, and I gently picked up its body and took it inside. I sensed the dragonfly held some deep significance related to the day's events, but I didn't understand how until weeks later.

I told Penelope about the vision that had foreshadowed KC's death and the appearance of the dragonfly, which I felt was more than a coincidence. Penelope explained it further to me.

"The apparent solidity of the physical reality we live in is an illusion. We actually live within a grid of multiple realities, which are happening simultaneously. Many times we are not aware of the different realities or dimensions until they intersect with one another. How a person reacts to the events going on in the moment influences how things will play out. Your scream shifted reality in that split instant, and KC was able to stay in physical reality. The dragonfly volunteered to die for KC so he could live longer."

Months later KC began showing signs of not feeling well. The vet proclaimed, "Your dog has a tumor wrapped around his aorta. He has cancer. There's a good chance he's dying." The vet said KC could undergo an operation but his chances were not good because of the location of the tumor. Chemotherapy and radiation were not an option for the same reason. In the meantime, because the tumor was cutting off the blood circulation from his heart, his lungs quickly filled up with fluid.

The thought of losing my animal friend horrified me. We had KC's lungs tapped to remove the excess fluid. The vet predicted the fluid would return, and warned me that the faster it returned, the worse it would be for KC. My husband, George, and I scrambled to find out what alternative therapies were available that could help. KC's time on Earth was running out.

We spent as much time with KC as possible, taking quiet walks and being with him in his favorite places. The day we decided to euthanize him, because he was drowning from the fluid in his lungs, was the saddest, hardest day of my life. KC resisted and tried to run out of the room. I held him tightly in my arms and told him I loved him, and then his spirit released from his body.

Despite the time to prepare, the emotional loss was devastating. For three months I couldn't tell people about KC's passing because I was in shock and it hurt so much not having him by my side. KC and I had been so intertwined for nine years that I had to figure out who I was without him.

A few months after his crossing, KC sent us two adorable kittens. I was grateful they were able to help me with my grief. A year later, Kobe Bear, another keeshond, came to us. I felt that Kobe was also a special gift from KC.

I kept the dragonfly, grateful that he had given me a few more months to prepare for KC's departure.

The circumstances surrounding an animal's death can be complex, filled with meaning and offering much to learn. By cultivating our intuitive sensing, we can learn how to glean rich realizations about the journey with our animal friends that can assist us in our evolution, even unto death. Ask your animal friends for signs of connection and be open to signs that come in surprising ways, as illustrated in the next story.

Another animal, who was also named KC, gave her human companions, Morgine and Jerry Jurdan, a sign and a spiritual gift as she left the Earth. Her departure was filled with bliss for Morgine and Jerry. Morgine tells the story:

We took our nineteen-year-old cat, KC, to the vet's office when she was ready to pass and asked for assistance. A year and a half previous to this, we had been told her thyroid needed radiation and her kidneys were failing. KC told us she wanted no veterinary treatment. We did gentle healing work, and she continued to live a happy and peaceful life during that time.

At Donna's veterinary office, we laid out a big red towel, lit red heart candles, and put out some red berries and a big red bow from a Christmas wreath, making an altar just as KC had requested. We played the songs she wanted. Donna found KC's thyroid enlarged and her kidneys extremely tender. KC was beginning to experience severe pain, and she wanted help in leaving.

First, Donna gave KC an anesthetic to help her relax. Jerry stepped outside to be in nature for a moment. I held KC in my arms. As Donna was giving the anesthetic, we began to hear KC shout for joy as she left her body. "I'm free! I feel so good!" She kept communicating how good it felt to be out of her body. Donna and I smiled.

As KC was leaving her body, Jerry saw a circular rainbow in the sky. A moment later, a long-haired black cat named Aisha came out of the bushes meowing and ushered Jerry back inside. With the final injection, I felt that KC was no longer in her body, but the room was filled with her spirit. I did not miss KC in that moment because I felt her presence all around me and knew she would be with us always.

4

Animal Choice and Purpose

*Master beings take the form of companion animals to assist people
through times of rapid spiritual expansion. These beings often come
into incarnation for specific reasons, and when their task is complete
they simply leave. My cat, Shoji, had come to assist me through
my illness, near death experience, and reorientation to the world.
He simply completed the job he had come to do and then
it was time for him to go.*

—Sharon Callahan

$\mathcal{M}$any animals make conscious choices about when, how, and where
they will die. The way they die is often related to their own function or
purpose in life. People might consider an accident involving the death
of an animal to be a tragedy, but it might actually be the animal's
choice, accompanied by a call to come to the other side, or spiritual
realm. To understand an animal's departure, especially a sudden or
unexpected one, it helps enormously to understand the design or purpose of their whole life and get in touch with them afterwards about
what happened.

Some animals are clear about why and when they departed in a
certain way, but others may be uncertain about the whole process of
dying and indecisive about whether it's their time to go. Animal clarity is influenced by the fears and actions of the people surrounding
them when they are dying. Consultations with people and their animal friends during the dying process and after death can bring so much

understanding. The communion and connection can alleviate confusion, guilt, and the misery of deep loss.

🐾 HUMAN EXPECTATIONS AND BELIEFS 🐾

I have been asked to communicate with many animals of various species after they have passed on. Religious or philosophical traditions may dictate that a certain path, kingdom, or state will appear as a being moves from the physical to the spiritual plane. I have found that each one has an individual experience. Although there are common experiences of life after death, there is much that is unique, according to a being's expectations and life choices.

Harold and Misty called me about their Pharaoh hound, Fara, who had recently been killed by a car in front of their home. When I contacted Fara, she communicated that she felt free and joyous as a spirit. She had literally run out of her body when she ran in front of the car. Her death was instantaneous. She left a split second before the impact and felt no pain and had no regrets. She said that she was only meant to be here for a short time as a dog. Her purpose had been to bring magic, joy, and lightness to people, and she felt she had fulfilled her commitment.

Misty was saddened but eager to get in touch with Fara, and she understood what had happened. Harold had a harder time. He was angry. The teacher of his religious philosophy decreed that dogs were subservient to humans and their purpose in life was to learn obedience to their human masters. Harold did not feel the dog had learned her lesson. Since Fara had not listened to him and ran into the street, Harold felt she needed to reincarnate as a dog again.

When I conferred with Fara about this, she asked me to convey her freedom, light, warmth, and happiness as a spiritual being to Harold and Misty. She was, indeed, wise, complete, and beautiful.

There is no one way of looking at the purposes, lives, and after-death experiences of individual beings that fits the infinity of variations we are able to create and experience as spirit. Spiritual experience cannot be pigeonholed to fit the human quest for hierarchical or neatly organized compartments.

I had a bantam chicken friend named P.J., who loved to sit on my knee and be cuddled, unlike most of the other chickens, who preferred to stay together in a flock. The bantam roosters found her attractive, with her fluffy black feathers and feathered feet, but she, unlike most of the other hens, resented their courting and mating activities.

One day, she told me she didn't want to be like the other chickens anymore. She wanted to live with me in the house, sit on my lap, and be my companion. Chicken droppings on the floor and furniture are not my idea of a nice house, so I tried to accommodate her wishes with other arrangements. She was not satisfied and told me she would prefer to be some other animal so she could live with me in the house. Then she proceeded to get sick, refusing to accept any treatment, and died.

P.J. got her wish. She contacted me awhile after her death and told me when and where I could find her as a cuddly, little hamster, who could live with me in the house.

ANIMAL CLARITY AND HUMAN AMBIVALENCE

People often find it hard when animals die young, feeling their life was cut off for no purpose or it was their fault for not caring for their animals well enough. I have communicated with many amazing beings who incarnate into animal bodies to bring people a burst of love, light, and connection with spirit, but who are on a sort of timetable to go back to their spiritual homes after a limited lifespan.

Sashi was a six-month-old kitten who was hit by a car, much to his human companions' grief. When I contacted him, he showed me he was filled with joy. He said that when he was alive, he sped around.

He literally couldn't stay in the body because of his high vibratory state. His human companions chuckled in agreement when he relayed the description of himself as a cat. He had to go, so he leapt in front of a car and zoomed out of his body, all the while showering his blessings on his former family.

Many people feel blessed by angelic beings like Sashi. These animals are wonderful, and they give so much love, peace, and light that people want to hold onto them. Count your blessings when beings like this come into your life. You must be doing something right! Appreciate them for who they are and acknowledge the wisdom they bring. They may be here for a short or long time, according to their purpose. Honor them and let go, knowing that you are always connected spiritually.

Animal communicator Sue Becker learned a lot about animal choice and purpose when she helped her clients with the dying process of their rescued kitten, Maggie May.

Maggie was lethargic and had a slightly swollen abdomen, which pointed to a developing case of feline infectious peritonitis (FIP), notoriously fatal in kittens. At first, the veterinarian did not suspect FIP because Maggie's symptoms were not consistent with this diagnosis. I used muscle-testing to check if it was FIP and also got a negative response. We were jubilant! As time went on, Maggie's illness became more evident and the vet confirmed the worst-case diagnosis of FIP. I asked Maggie what her illness was all about.

"I bring lessons. I am impacting many people and animal beings during my short life. I bring opportunities for patience, for learning to let go, for the vet to learn, and to bring enjoyment and pleasure to others. Sweet life can be hard and painful, but this is temporary and the benefits are great. I accept the circumstances of this lifetime and leave it as easily as shutting my eyes. It's harder for some people to understand the simplicity of the process. I survive as a being of light with my physical body discarded."

"But your body is so beautiful," I told her.

"It's the beauty of my true being that you see and believe to be the physical body," Maggie said. "It's my time and choice to leave. My short life reflects the transience of physical life. A full-span human life is as short in the view of eternity as mine appears to you. Yet, there are immense lessons to be learned and evolution that can occur during a brief period of time. As a cat, I teach and show people the process, and I am honored to do so."

Maggie asked for help to leave when her humans were ready to let go. She gave me this message to relay:

"Tell them not to grieve. I am being set free. I am in control of my experience. The situation has been my choice, and there is absolutely no resistance or struggle on my part. When there is no resistance or struggle on their part, *their* light will become brighter as will mine. Tell them they can connect with me whenever they wish after I am physically gone. I will be available. Tell them to ask in their hearts whether I am happy, and they will know. I thank them for their kindness, generosity, and love. This has eased my path. We have made a connection that will never be broken, although they may not always be aware of it. Ultimately, we are all part of each other. Remind them of our oneness."

I asked Maggie why my muscle test indicated she did not have FIP and would live.

"Your skills *are* trustworthy," she replied. "At that time, the response was correct for *you*, although not accurate in reality. It allowed you to continue with the tasks at hand, and it allowed my humans to do the same. In your heart, you had the knowledge that it was FIP. However, you allowed the vet's opinion and your own hope to sway you, evidenced by your jubilation at the result. A detached outlook is necessary."

From this example, we can see that even experienced animal communicators can err in receiving information when they have let their own desires for a certain outcome cloud their true perception. When you practice receiving your animal friend's communications, do your best to put aside your own preconceived notions about what is happening. Often, the sign of a true communication from the animal is that it's surprising and doesn't match your own ideas. Each animal has his or her own way of thinking, feeling, perceiving, and reason for being. Each time you communicate with an animal can be a great discovery of another culture.

I did a consultation with a wonderful Newfoundland dog named Mr. B., who was quite ill. He was breathing heavily, could barely move, and the vet had diagnosed advanced hip dysplasia. Mr. B. was a spiritually advanced being and knew exactly what he was doing. He fondly guided his human companion, Catherine. He told me he was ready to go and felt it would be within a few days. Both Mr. B. and Catherine experienced a resurgence of energy after the consultation, and with veterinary treatment for an infection in his hips, Mr. B. was able to walk again.

A month later, Catherine planned to attend my basic "How to Communicate with Animals" course. She called me the night before the course, unsure if Mr. B. could make it.

After she called, I felt Mr. B. would be able to get there. It took Catherine a long time to gradually move her large, ailing dog into the car. When she arrived, Mr. B. couldn't make it over to where the other dogs and people were assembled for the outdoor course, and he lay in the grass near the car about fifty feet away.

As we did the course exercises, some participants got perceptions and communications about Mr. B's spiritual state. After a few hours, Mr. B. left his body, which was a profound experience for everyone. A few of us experienced Mr. B. in spirit as quite playful and glad to be leaving during this auspicious time.

Catherine sat quietly beside Mr. B's body, while the rest of us continued the course exercises. The other dogs present were not disturbed by the death, and Mr. B. continued to participate spiritually in the course, with Catherine joining in again later.

As we can see from the example of Mr. B., we might surprise our-selves by our own response to death when we spiritually attune to the animal who is leaving. Instead of a tragic experience, death can be an exaltation of spirit for all involved.

Karina Heuzeröth, an animal communicator who trained with me in Germany, had a female German shepherd named Afra. This example shows how prior knowledge from an animal about his or her impend-ing death can still be shocking and hard to accept.

Afra was my companion during horse rides. She was proud of her phys-ical condition, and people always thought she was much younger than she actually was. When I started to work as an animal communicator, Afra once told me that she never wanted to become an old, suffering dog. She said emphatically that when she was no longer able to be really active, she wanted to leave this world. She sent me images of being in a car accident.

As Afra grew older, I tried to forget what she had communicated about her death. When she was eleven years old, she had problems climbing stairs and could no longer jump into the car without someone supporting her hind legs. She still enjoyed walks, although she could not accompany me on longer rides because her joints would ache afterwards. She continued to look like a much younger dog.

On September 7, 2004, the divine plan Afra had chosen took its course. When I led the horses to their meadow, usually Afra went right behind them. This time it was different. I heard a car approaching very quickly. When I looked back at Afra, I was surprised to see her going onto the road. I called to her, but she just gave me a look that said, "Now!"

The young man in the car was driving so fast that Afra was dead in a split second. She didn't suffer at all, but it was a horrible situation for me. I had the horses on lead ropes and needed to take them back to their pasture. Shocked and crying, my whole body was trembling.

I immediately got from Afra that now she had what she wanted. She had fulfilled her chosen fate.

During the first summer without Afra's physical presence, I was finally able to say goodbye to her. I went to a little lake where we had often gone swimming and shared profound times in the surrounding forest. While I missed Afra, I was so grateful for everything she had given and taught me.

When some animals leave, even when they have clearly decided to go, it can be confusing for both the humans and the other animal companions left behind, even when they communicate with each other spiritually.

Banjo was a ten-year-old terrier whose human companion, Diana, called me after he had drowned in the family pool. It was an incredible experience to contact Banjo. The dog said he saw a large oval light on the other side of the swimming pool. He had been seeing it for several weeks for brief moments. The night he died, he had felt called to the other side of the pool. He *knew* he had to follow the light. He was hardly aware of it when his body fell into the pool. There were several seconds of physical struggle, but he was lifted out of his body and continued "walking" towards the light as a spirit.

Banjo appeared to me as an angelic presence surrounded by other beings of light. He was sending his family on Earth light and warmth. He felt like this state was a continuance of his role as a dog companion. Diana said she had always felt Banjo was an angel.

For Lisa, the female terrier in the family, Banjo's departure was confusing. When he was alive, he had been the family guardian and the "star." Banjo communicated to her after his death, telling her to take care of the family. Lisa told me she didn't know how; that was his job. I advised her human friends to acknowledge her as a wonderful companion, and let her work out a role that was comfortable for her in the family, knowing she had their assurance and approval.

🐾 THE CYCLE OF LIFE 🐾

The manner of death that an animal chooses, and the way they live their lives, can cause profound shifts in the people around them, often giving them major boosts along their spiritual paths. Sue Hopple tells how her cat and a coyote taught her about the great cycle of life when she was beginning to learn how to communicate with animals:

Oscar, our huge black and white, eleven-year-old cat had severe arthritis in his back hips and knees from injuries he had sustained in his younger days. He walked with a limp. I tried different medications and natural remedies to help him move better and dull his pain. In the beginning, it seemed as though some of these methods worked. As time went on, however, we both grew tired of the medications. I knew Oscar was growing extremely weary when I had to set up a litter box in the house because it was too difficult for him to manage the cat door, and he was no longer able to climb onto the bed.

I felt in my heart that Oscar was preparing to leave his body, and I cherished every moment we had together. Finally, it came time for me to tell Oscar that if he felt he needed to move on, it was all right with me. I was holding him close to my heart when I told him, and I could feel the vibration of his purr throughout my entire body. I went to sleep that night feeling comforted, never dreaming of the events that would follow the next morning.

Around 5:30 AM, I was awakened by the barking of Snap, one of our four dog companions. We have five acres, and the top two acres are fenced with non-climb fencing so the dogs don't run off and the wild animals don't get in. On this morning, everything felt different.

I went out on the deck overlooking our property. Just on the other side of the fence was a pale gray coyote. He looked up at me and then circled around a large clump of bushes with a noticeable limp. "Black cat" flashed through my mind. In the same moment that I saw the coyote, a mother deer, with her two young fawns close behind her, [was] also running across the fields to the west. It made me immediately think "Oh, a sign of new beginnings and birth."

As I was walking back to the house, the coyote appeared again in another part of the yard. "How odd," I thought, "Why hasn't he left the area?" He again looked straight at me with his piercing eyes, and continued to limp away. It felt like he was trying to either tell me something or trick me.

During the next hour, as I fed the horses and did other morning chores, the coyote was still popping up around our fencing. Oscar's name did occur to me many times, but I put it aside. When Snap continued barking at the coyote at the end of our driveway behind the gate, I went out to meet with the coyote. He ran across the street into a large grassy field and then bent his head down as he pulled on something. My heart sank because I knew he was eating. I yelled at him, and he ran off into the field. I chased after him and stopped at the place where he had bent down. There in that spot lay Oscar. His neck had been broken and part of his chest ripped open.

My heart sank in sorrow and disbelief. "How could this happen?" I thought. I knew Oscar wanted to go, but I never thought it would be this way. I screamed out in pain and grief. My husband, hurt about Oscar, shot at the coyote but missed. As the coyote ran with speed off into the hills, we noticed he had no visible limp.

At that moment, I knew Oscar had set up his death. Oscar knew we did not have the heart to take him to the vet to be put down. My blame for the coyote left, yet it was still heartbreaking to see Oscar's body torn apart. I could hear him telling me to stop looking at his body like that, because it was no longer him. I felt a sense of relief and joy coming from Oscar. My husband made a comment that he also felt different toward the coyote, feeling in his heart that it was Oscar's wish.

In order for Oscar to be caught by the coyote, he had to limp a long way down our driveway and crawl underneath the gate. This must have been quite painful. I began to understand more about what had happened, but I was still not happy about how Oscar had chosen to end his life. Looking back, I realize how odd the behavior of the coyote really was, because I know in a normal situation the coyote would have either left the area or dragged Oscar's body away. It was as if the coyote was trying to tell me what had happened. I know that if I had never found Oscar's body, I would have wandered all over the countryside looking for him.

All that day, Oscar came into my thoughts, saying, "I'm okay. I have comfort and joy, and you should, too." However, as the days passed I still felt haunted by the coyote's behavior the morning Oscar died. In my quest for understanding animal communication and my own journey, I had to know the whole story.

A few days later, I headed to Point Reyes, California for an advanced course in animal communication with Penelope Smith. I was hoping that during the course I would get more answers about the coyote and his meaning for me.

On the second day of the class, we were doing an exercise on "being present." Before the next assignment, I asked Penelope to clarify the incident with Oscar and the coyote. Her response was, "You are ready to answer this yourself. Ask the coyote your question during the next exercise."

Her confidence in the connection between humans and animals was overwhelming. In that instant, I knew I would receive the answer to my questions. I became fully present and asked the coyote if he was a trickster, or whether his limp that morning had been to tell me about Oscar. The coyote replied:

"We trick to survive when we have to. My limp was to tell you it was Oscar, the cat with the limp. I moved around your property to get your attention and to get you to see where Oscar lay. I had to keep an eye on his body, because foxes were waiting to take him off. Oscar wanted you to know what happened to him, although it's not quite how you saw him leave his body. I felt the need to eat him to own the kill. It's a cycle of life. Don't be afraid of this process. I am the one who has watched you before. I am old and wise. I work alone. I was an old Indian in a time past. You have asked about your past heritage, and you will be receiving answers as you go on your journey. When I am around you, it's sacred ground. I could get one of your cats at any time and do not. This was a request from Oscar and it was all part of a plan."

As I read this to Penelope that day, she replied, "You got it. You got it all!"

In that moment, time again stood still for me. I had been blessed with an event that no person on Earth could have taught me. The Great Spirit answered my prayers and through our beloved companion, Oscar, brought new meaning to my life. I also felt such a sense of compassion for the coyote who had granted Oscar's wishes. Then I realized there was also great significance in the deer and the two fawns I had seen that same morning because they symbolized the birth of a new beginning.

Not only was new light shed on my path, but it helped me to understand the great cycle of all life. It's our ignorance of this cycle that causes continual sorrow and pain. Through Oscar the cat and the coyote, I found comfort in the cycle of life and was able to rejoice in the fact that we are all connected.

🐾 HELPING HUMANS EVOLVE 🐾

The lives of animals are gifts to us, but as some people gratefully discover, so are their deaths. Often animals are here for a larger purpose than only to serve as our companions. In their dying, they are often working with larger forces and a piece of the planetary task of spiritual evolution for us all. They can move a lot of energy, clearing old patterns for many—or even all—beings on Earth. They give us a great gift of light when they go, and they often open portals to different levels of awareness or to different dimensions. Practice being open to receiving the gifts of your animal friends when they depart.

Early in 2002, Reya, my eight-year-old female Afghan hound, let me know her job with me was done and she would be leaving. Within a few weeks, she became fussier with her food and began to lose weight and energy. The vet diagnosed kidney failure and was dubious at this stage about whether treatment in the hospital would help her. I talked it over with Reya. She didn't want treatment but wanted to make her transition quietly at home with me.

I stayed to be with her instead of leaving on March 22 for the whale journey I was scheduled to facilitate in the Dominican Republic. We spent the time of passage in a mystical, rose quartz light and heart communion, receiving many spiritual gifts as she gracefully walked her way out of this realm and into her starry light home.

On March 27, the first day of Passover, the day of liberation, Reya left for the spirit realm with the Ancient Grandmothers (planetary ancestor spirits) during the full moon light. I felt her opening a doorway to incredible light energies for the whole planet.

Beings who embody advanced consciousness of their union with all life may influence the weather and other natural phenomena in their passage from Earth. The universe seems to collaborate to acknowledge their impact and importance to us all in this way. These signs can act as confirmation of connection and support to those who knew these beings and mourn their passing. These phenomena also show the aliveness, awareness, and connection of all forms of life.

I told Reya's many friends and students to look for a glow like the Northern Lights coming through the atmosphere wherever they were—luminescent aqua, blue, and violet with tinges of rose quartz pink. The sky conspired in demonstrating Reya's magic. My sweetheart angel ray of light was blessing us all in her passage.

I gave her body back to Mother Earth, placing it a hole she had helped to dig for several summers underneath the bay tree where she had enjoyed the earth's coolness. I felt all was in Divine Order. My aching heart was full of the joy and love of Reya's precious being.

Many people who had known Reya recognized her beautiful soul purpose of radiating light, sweet, star-child energy to open the hearts of all she met. In departing this realm, she deepened the impact of her life's gift. Upon hearing of her death, many people paid her tribute.

Another of my animal friends, a cockatiel who renamed himself Pirouette, had a huge impact on people in life and in death. It was

October 1982, and I was living in Los Angeles. A client called for a consultation about her cockatiel. She was disturbed because the two-year-old bird screamed in the middle of the night and woke her up, no matter how she covered the cage or yelled at the bird to stop. This went on night after night. When I arrived, human and cockatiel were both frazzled. The woman had recently gone through a big relationship breakup and was experiencing deep emotional distress. Although I felt I could help them handle the situation, she asked me if I would just take the cockatiel (then called Pishta), cage and all.

I took the bird home, and thus began our twenty-two-year relationship. Right at the start, he indicated his new name would be Pirouette. He never screamed during the night again. The woman had insulted him and I wanted to shift that feeling, so I said to him often in a cheerful voice, "You're terrific, Pirouette; you're terrific."

Within days, after never talking before in his life, he was bobbing up and down, dancing on his branches, and chortling with gusto, saying: "You're terrific, Pirouette; you're terrific."

Next, I told him, "I love you, Pirouette. Thank you, Pirouette. You're terrific," punctuated with kissing sounds. He added these happy phrases and kissing sounds to his repertoire, along with the first song I whistled for him: "Yankee Doodle." I got some bird training recordings so he could expand his repertoire without me having to talk to him repetitively. He didn't like the recordings and only wanted to hear my voice.

I told him I couldn't keep talking and whistling endlessly, but I would turn on the classical music radio station and he could pick out his own tunes. Within a short time, Pirouette was whistling recognizable phrases from symphonies. After awhile, he tired of listening to classical music and decided that jazz was more to his liking. He began to improvise and construct his own endlessly varying melodies, often interspersing them with the familiar "Yankee Doodle," while dancing on his branches or the bottom of his cage.

We sang, talked, and danced together for years. With dignity, grace, wisdom, and joy, he helped many people open and deepen their telepathic connection with animals at the many basic and advanced courses I conducted. My former husband, Michel Sherman, played classical guitar and lute, and Pirouette assisted him with musical inspiration, eventually "collaborating" in producing the musical recording *The Earth Speaks*.

After Michel and I parted ways, Pirouette eventually lived full-time with Michel, except to visit me when Michel was out of town or occasionally to continue helping me teach advanced courses. Pirouette slowed down in his elder years, rarely dancing, singing, or flying as he had done when he was younger.

Michel sent me an e-mail on my birthday, October 28, 2004, telling me Pirouette had passed away. I received it a few days later during a shamanic retreat, and I shared this news with the group. We held a ceremony in honor of Pirouette around a newly planted, baby giant Sequoia tree. We gathered around the tree with two of his tail feathers and sang and chanted, rattled and drummed. Pirouette appeared in spirit and "sat" on top of a tall, dead pine tree, shining down on us.

He departed from this world on the night of a full moon lunar eclipse. That night brought in a wave of soft energy to aid in our planetary evolutionary movement to love incarnate. Pirouette carried the wave further and wider through this plane and beyond. During the ceremony, many vultures flew around the tree where Pirouette was perched in spirit. Along with Pirouette, they carried the energy, spreading it over the world.

Sharing his passing so deeply with kindred spirits, united with the Elder Spirits in our retreat, helped me to pass through the wave of grief and loss, and celebrate his spiritual reunion with "All That Is." I am grateful to have lived with Master Pirouette for so many years. He helped many people awaken to their true selves and remember how to connect and communicate with all beings. I am honored that he chose my birth time for his passing.

Yohinta was a cat with fierce purpose in life and strong resolution in death. Her dying was celebrated in a manner that honored her life mission.

Many people knew Yohinta as a wonderful, warm, spirited teacher. Working with many students throughout her sixteen years, she specialized in helping those who were struggling with emotional issues. She moved students to tears of cleansing and realization with her patient, loving, and knowing presence. She also did not put up with nonsense. Once, when a student was invalidating her own ability to communicate with animals, Yohinta pointedly batted and grabbed the woman's hand with her teeth, which effectively reminded the student of her own telepathic connection.

Yohinta reflected a full range of deep emotions. A loving soul, she was also known for her intense passion and stubbornness, signaled by the orange, lightning-shaped mark above and between her eyes on the dark fur of her forehead. She scarred my living room rugs with her persistent scratching over the years, despite the fact that she also used the available scratching posts. None of the other cats violated the no-scratching rule. Regardless of my protests about the marred rugs, she just had to dig in to this woolly base of support and comfort. I surrendered to appreciating her joy and the artistically shredded design, now part of her legacy.

As a fiery, tortoise shell cat, Yohinta suffered persistent allergy-based scratching, starting at three years of age, that a multitude of holistic remedies did not ease but infrequent prednisone shots alleviated. Otherwise, only when her attention was fully occupied and her adrenalin was activated—by helping others through their stress or being in stressful situations herself (such as after fire destroyed our home in October 1995)—did she cease chewing, licking, and scratching her coat. During these times, Yohinta's coat would return to its shining, thick luxury.

We were completely intertwined with each other when she was a kitten. However, she never completely forgave me for leaving home when I had to travel. After I returned, she would ignore me or deliberately walk out the door in a huff and be gone for hours or even days.

On my last return home before her death, I was moved by Yohinta's change of attitude. Although she was quite weak, she came over to where I was sitting on the rug and greeting the other animals. Purring loudly, she gave me a tender, loving welcome and asked to be held and stroked.

As her body deteriorated during the last few years of her life, I asked her, if possible, to hold off dying while I was away teaching so I could be with her during her transition. When I left for Brazil on May 2, 2004, I kissed her good-bye, feeling that she wouldn't be able to honor my request. My former student and now friend, Starr Taovil, was able to housesit for me, and I couldn't have asked a better person to be with Yohinta during this sacred time.

Yohinta was doing deep Mother Earth work during her last weeks. Thin and bloated, she would slowly walk outside in the sun, sit on a mound of earth, and channel dark energies of planetary karmic strife that would be washed and integrated through Mother Earth. It was so heart opening to be around her in her delicate and prayerful state.

I asked Starr to call my traveling companion's cell phone if necessary for emergencies. For some technical reason, phone messages didn't come through to us in Brazil until May 12. When there was a message from Starr, I knew it had to be about Yohinta.

When I called Starr back, I found out that Yohinta had passed away on May 10 at 2:36 PM. I was surprised that I had received no telepathic clue, although that morning, just hours before I got Starr's two-day-old phone message, I had experienced visions of Yohinta as a kitten and thought about our life together. Later, it became clear that Yohinta had been busy during this time and did not feel a need to contact me right away. I felt deep regret that I couldn't be there for her in her final days.

I had asked Sherman, our orange tabby, wizard cat, to take care of Yohinta while I was away. Before I left, he had been bringing her the gophers that he patiently hunted and she ravenously ate. They seemed to provide her with the lifeblood energy she needed to do her final work on Earth. I asked him to continue to bring her live food as long as she needed the nourishment. Starr reported that Sherman brought Yohinta gophers as she rested outside in the sun, and licked her forehead lovingly as she ate.

Yohinta couldn't eat or drink during her last two days. During her final hour, Sherman brought her two gophers and a rabbit, and then he quietly sat next to her. These animal offerings were an expression of his deep love. The rabbit was a special blessing to her from him, and the wild animal friends gave themselves willingly to ease her suffering and accompany her on her soul journey.

As I grieved and felt guilty about not being present for her, I got some relief and clarity when I read an astrology report for May 10. It was the last day of the waning moon, which is a day of dying and letting go, just before the new beginning brought by the new moon. I realized that leaving her body on this day made it easier for Yohinta to have a gentle, smooth departure.

As Yohinta grew weaker, Starr attended to her with the greatest love, surrounding her with lilies, roses, and flower essences. Yohinta cried out at 4:00 AM on the final day. She wanted to be held for a long time, despite the tenderness of her frail body. During her final hour, she asked to be taken all around our land, the Floating Island of Peace, stopping at favorite spots such as the Fairy Ring, which overlooks the surrounding countryside, and the flowering garden outside my office where she often relaxed. Sherman led the walk. Dog companions, Buddha Boy and Belinda, followed.

After the walk, Yohinta asked Starr to sit on the bench in the afternoon sun, facing the tallest mountain in the area and the ocean, close to the spot where Pasha, our Afghan hound, had left about eleven years previously. Starr held Yohinta in her arms and sang her a song; Sherman sat on the bench next to them; and Buddha Boy and Belinda sat on the ground facing Starr and Yohinta. With great reverence from all the family surrounding her, Yohinta took a final, deep, relaxed breath of ocean air, and painlessly expired. Her soul left to the south, in the same direction as Pasha and Reya, our Afghans, had departed.

Starr prepared a beautiful area with sacred objects and placed Yohinta's body on her special pillow. She and her partner, Art, prayed and sang as all the animals sat nearby. The animals touched their noses to Yohinta and sat down again. Starr and Art prepared Yohinta's body, with great respect, to be kept in the freezer so I could perform the burial ceremony when I returned in eight days. Starr felt honored that Yohinta had shared this time with her, and reported that Yohinta had helped her complete unresolved feelings about her mother's death.

Before I returned on May 18, Yohinta showed me how she was expanding as a spirit. Heyoka, her dear cat companion, who had died five years previously at the same age as Yohinta died, expanded with her. He had been awaiting Yohinta's return to spirit and now felt exalted in union with her.

Buddha Boy was saddened by Yohinta's passing. Sherman was busy supporting everyone through the journey, but he also felt personal loss at her leaving. Sherman, just three months younger than Yohinta, had been her playmate throughout the years. Belinda, although new to the household, also felt sadness.

We comforted each other when I arrived home. As I walked Starr to her car and talked about Yohinta, a lone vulture flew over us. I could feel the spirit of Yohinta and the Ancient Grandmothers with her.

I prepared Yohinta's body for burial soon after I arrived home. Her ears and eyes were crumpled (Starr mentioned that her eyes were swollen when she died), but her fur was still soft. Gratefully placing her body in the Earth next to Heyoka's grave, I covered it with roses and other flowers, sage and other herbs, feathers, and a heart amulet, along with the beads and a cross that Starr had wrapped with her body. I tucked her favorite treats of carob and tortilla chips under her chin, another gift to honor her life. Buddha, Sherman, and Belinda all reverently attended the ceremony. I cried, sang, and spent a long time feeling all that Yohinta had meant to me in life and how beautiful she was, and still is, in spirit. I recalled my favorite nicknames for her: Bebe Chat (French for Baby Cat), Yoyo Buttons, Botones (Spanish for Buttons). I covered her grave with flowers, a stone marker, an amethyst cluster, a cat figurine, and a large vulture feather standing tall.

I am writing this a few days after the burial. Our family is grieving quietly in communion with Yohinta and all of life around us. I feel our "atmospheric" energies fluctuating and realigning Buddha Boy, Belinda, Sherman, and I are holding each other tenderly in the wake of this gentle tidal wave. How strange, sad, and moving it is when a dear companion leaves. It also feels odd to have only one cat companion after three have left in the last five years. What great teachers all of them have been.

Ceremonial honoring of our animal friends' life and passing (described in these examples or created through individual inspiration) can bring us into deep communion with them, uplifting our spirits and helping us to evolve and receive animals' incredible blessings.

Laurie Moore was part of the collective karmic clearing work that Yohinta accomplished during her dying time.

Visions and awakenings of unconditional love, bliss, and joy have been taking my heart, but I have also felt attacked by terrorist images. I sometimes misunderstand these images, believing them to indicate something personally inadequate about myself. They come as visions from some other source, pictures sent out into the cosmos that have entered my receivers. I have been plagued by them. I have also been approached by clients who work with the light in various healing profession and who have had similar difficulties.

After reading the story of Yohinta's passage, published in *Species Link* magazine, I felt a need to communicate with her. Since then, Yohinta has guided me. She teaches me patience, peace, and trust. The terrorist images are from the collective mind, and they need to be acknowledged and released into the light for conversion. When I match their energy with a higher frequency level of love and gratitude, and tell them, "I forgive you. Thank you. And now you may go," I am cleansed. They are collective karma pointing to the places in me that need to be tuned up with kind patience to greater light.

Yohinta shows me there is no time like the present to be part of the love clearing. Now is the time to love and allow all that is not love to pass through in transition back to its original love source until only love is perceived.

People are often distraught by the physical aspect of animals who are in trouble or dying. They may lack understanding of the spiritual purposes behind these situations.

In 1985, some people who were worried about the slaughter of dolphins in the nets of Japanese tuna fishermen called me and asked me to tell the dolphins to stay away from the nets. When I telepathically contacted the dolphins at a distance, they communicated that they had their own purpose and mission regarding the slaughter. They told me that humans needed their blood and death in order to shock human consciousness and wake them up to taking positive action before they destroyed all life on the planet. They explained that dolphins and whales throughout history have been spiritual friends and guides to humans. Because many people would not listen to peaceful spiritual messages and learn from their water brothers and sisters' harmonious example, they needed a more forceful communication to reach people. If the dolphins had to sacrifice their bodies to arouse positive change, they were willing to do it.

The actions of dolphins and whales throughout the years have moved countless people to try to save them, and also to change humanity's attitude and approach toward their fellow creatures, the ocean, and the Earth. Decades later, after many more dolphin and whale emissaries have contacted people and sacrificed their lives, more can be done in raising human consciousness so that our cetacean brothers and sisters do not have to die to help us awaken. In their great benevolence, they wish us to evolve and end our slaughter of other species and each other.

5

Shelter and Rescued Animals

Don't worry about the animals. All beings, even unto death and through great suffering, can really take care of themselves.

—Jean Mahoney, former animal rescuer

*T*his chapter addresses some common questions and issues about animal death and suffering posed by people who rescue animals and who work in animal shelters.

1. Why are some animals in a shelter?

On a broad level, the animals are in shelters due to human ignorance and irresponsibility in not getting companion animals spayed and neutered. There is a surplus of animals who do not have homes.

Animals, including humans, incarnate in order to live the biological program or purpose of their physical body, while also having a sense of their true spiritual nature and why they are here. Most domestic animals want to be companions to people. Since they, like the rest of us, are not consciously in control of everything in life, and animals are not always treated well by people, they can end up abused, abandoned, and exterminated. Life on Earth can be tough.

Some animals find people and life overwhelming. They feel they have made a mistake. They peeked at the world through a dog or cat form and have now decided they want to leave. Others did not know they would die so soon, but there just wasn't room for them with people.

I learned about how animals sometimes choose death when I met a three-year-old female German shepherd, Sara, who was extremely aggressive toward people and other dogs. Her human companions had tried various means of training and controlling her, with no success, and were faced with having to exterminate the dog.

When I talked to Sara, she seemed quite serious and said she was here to guard her human family, whom she loved. She felt it was reasonable to bite other people or dogs she didn't like. She was well trained, obedient, and loving with her human companions, but she had a strong will regarding her mode of guarding them. Unlike some people, who unconsciously or consciously encourage and admire aggressive behavior in their dogs, Sara's human companions had done everything they could to work with her and discourage her aggressive behavior.

Sara was not willing to change, so I recommended muzzling her. Her human companions knew she could get out of a muzzle, so they didn't feel it would work. I explained to Sara that her family was considering exterminating her if she did not change her ways. Unlike most dog companions, she was unmoved. She said she already understood what would happen. She had a job to do and if she was put down, then her job would be done. She did not wish to talk further about it.

While this appeared straightforward from the dog's point of view, it certainly was hard on the humans involved. They didn't want Sara to spend her life on a chain or kenneled, and they did not want to risk their dog hurting other people or dogs. It looked like Sara had made her choice.

Some animals may have a karmic reason for ending up in an animal shelter. They are seeking to understand an old pattern or fulfill a previous debt. On a visit to a zoo, I saw a leopard pacing and yowling pitifully in a small cage. I felt his despair and humiliation. The zoo was switching over to large, naturalistic habitats for the animals, but he was still stuck in a cage. I moved away to sit on a bench and communicate with him, because his misery was overwhelming. I asked him why he was in such a predicament. He relayed to me images of his last lifetime when he was a man who poached animals illegally, including leopards. In this life he had landed in the opposite role to pay his dues and understand another side to life.

2. What can we do while visiting a shelter to ease the fears of the animals we are unable to rescue?

Let the animals know they can visualize to the universe, and to the people who visit, that they want a home and are willing to serve and be happy. This can help them get out of the shelter. When animals visualize exactly what kind of home they want and who they want to live with, they start to attract the people who are meant to adopt them.

Some animals in shelters are locked in old trauma and unable to reach out. They may have difficulty changing from their depressed state to imagining having a good life. They may want to die, or they may succumb to the fear within and around them. Send love and blessings to animals who are about to die, and remind them of their true nature as spirits. Encourage them to choose a better situation the next time around.

I have held basic courses at Humane Societies, during which I have asked the students to work with animals who are fearful of people and feel they will never be adopted. When the students communicated with and understood the animals, the negative attitudes of the animals began to clear up. Then they were able to visualize exactly what they wanted. Even some of the hardest to place animals had found homes by the end of the course.

3. Do the animals know where they will go when they pass on?

Many have glimpses of other realms or remember where they came from. Some do not remember until they are separated from their bodies.

4. Do animals feel the same physical and emotional pain as humans? Does nature provide natural painkillers so they can cope better and survive?

Individual beings of any species have different sensitivities and reactions to pain. All animals can suffer physically and emotionally, although different species have different responses to painful stimuli. For example, many cats purr when they are injured or ill. Their purring acts as a sedative, releasing endorphins in the brain that actually help them endure pain.

When animals, including humans, are faced with severe stress or imminent death, shock and numbness usually take over, helping them detach from pain. When pounced on by a predator, most animals leave their bodies and either don't feel the impact or they release at impact. If the predator does not immediately kill the animal, the prey animals are usually out of the body, in a state of shock, detachment, or unconsciousness, and numb to physical sensation, even if their physical bodies continue to struggle. If their bodies are not killed and they recover from injury, their spirits usually return after awhile and the animals are able to feel physical sensation again.

The emotional pain in a shelter situation or the mass crowding of factory farming can create communal terror and misery that makes the prospect of dying horrible. Not knowing what is going to happen, while feeling the fear and confusion of the other animals, can make it a gruesome way to go, mitigated only by awareness and reconnection with self as spirit and a detachment from the body.

Death by injection is usually quick and painless, unless it's preceded by confusion about what's happening. Killing domestic animals because of overpopulation is not a happy prospect, even if certain individuals are aware of their reasons for dying this way.

5. *Do shelter animals have guardian angels to guide and comfort them?*
All of the living beings I have known appear to have guardian angels, or spiritual guides, and friends who are available to help when they are asked.

6. *Are animals sometimes surprised (as people have been reported to be) when they meet with sudden death?*
I have met animals who hang around their bodies, wondering what happened, even waiting to see if their bodies will get up again. Whenever

I see animals lying dead by the side of the road, I check to see if their spirits are okay. If they are still around, I let them know their former bodies are dead and they can move on. This is something that anyone can do. It's comforting for the animals and for us.

Part of the mystery and game of being alive is not knowing ahead of time what is going to happen, even if you designed your overall life plan before you incarnated and chose your path step by step. Forgetting what you knew when you were in spirit creates surprises and challenges for you during physical life.

Diane called me about her six-year-old dog, Beanie, who had been euthanized by mistake by a vet on Diane's order to put down her sixteen-year-old dog, who was blind and arthritic. Diane had been away when the vet came and could not understand how he made a mistake between the two dogs. Not only was she shocked, but Beanie was stunned. He was hanging around, wanting to come back. Diane was planning to get a new dog, so Beanie said he would come back to her, and, in effect, continue the life that was cut short.

Abigail, a domestic rabbit who lived outdoors, was grazing in a field when a hawk swooped down for her. She flew out of her body as the hawk struck. When we spoke with her, she was still flying because it was so much fun! She was even considering coming back as a hawk. Her sudden, unexpected death had opened up a new perspective on life.

7. Do animals know—by sensing in a way we can't understand— that death is all around them in the shelters? Is this why some of them seem depressed? Do they just give up?

Most animals know what's going on around them because they are in tune with their senses and able to receive thoughts telepathically. They may not understand exactly what's happening, how it will affect them, or believe it's going to happen to them. They may choose to hope for something better or deny the painful reality. They may get depressed, fearful, or resigned, or detached and peaceful. Hopefully, as more shelters shift into "no kill" status, animals will not have to feel the threat of imminent death around them in their place of rescue.

8. Some people work with feral cats by trapping and spaying and neutering them, and then releasing them in locations where they will receive food. Should this continue, or would it be more humane to euthanize them? Do cats in this type of living situation have emotional needs that are not being met?

Obviously, it's more ethical and humane to spay and neuter than to kill the surplus animals. Many cats prefer to be wild and are quite happy in a tended feral situation. Others have a purpose to be with people and want to be close to them and share their homes. Spending time quietly with these cats, observing what makes them comfortable, and listening to them as much as possible will help support them emotionally.

9. How can people who care for animals in shelters accept and feel better about what is happening to the animals?

From a higher or broader perspective, all forms and energies come and go in this physical plane. Everything transforms and spirit goes on. All beings who incarnate face physical death. Each individual has his or her purpose and his or her time, no matter how transitory. From the view of spirit, energies and physical forms are like modeling clay or artist paint—the materials of creation. Becoming them and detaching from them are part of life in this plane. A truth relayed in Buddhism is that suffering is caused by attachment to form and non-acceptance of the transitory nature of all things in this plane.

Obviously, as incarnate beings, we have an emotional stake in what happens here. Without caring and compassion about what goes on with other living beings, there is little joy in living. Living beings make their own choices about their lives in one fashion or another, even if they then "forget" or deny their own choices. You may be able to help others become conscious of the choices that create suffering and help them create harmony and joy, or you may be able to lift them out of terrible situations and help them to live happier lives. Help those who want and can accept your help in the manner that feels best to you, without burning yourself out in the process.

I once was driving back from teaching near Fresno, California, and got behind a huge truck full of chickens crammed into small cages. It was awful seeing them packed in like that. As I passed and looked at the side of the truck, I saw a dead chicken with her neck and head hanging out through the bars. I burst into tears because I felt the suffering of all those beings inside the truck. As I drove and sobbed, I asked the spirits of all the chickens on the truck, and all of the animals who have ever suffered at the hands of humans, to forgive us for our lack of understanding and callousness. I prayed for forgiveness and that humans would one day be more understanding and kinder to animals. I felt that my prayers increased my compassion toward the animals involved and might help bring the end of suffering a bit closer.

Whenever you experience animals suffering, particularly in instances where you can do nothing at that moment to relieve their suffering, you can pray and visualize relief and happiness for all the beings involved, including those who are causing the suffering. In this way, we can contribute good energy to the situation in the hopes it will change. We also help ourselves emotionally and spiritually in the process. Numerous studies have demonstrated the practical effectiveness of prayer and positive thinking.

10. Because some people are so sensitive to the situation of animals in shelters, could it be that they experienced the same thing in a past life? Do we move back and forth between being human and being other animals?
I have found in my experience of counseling thousands of humans and other species that a passion or major concern in a being's life has some past life connection or thread. It may be that you have been trying to help animals for lifetimes, or you are trying to make up for having hurt them in the past. An overriding concern can involve

individual incidents that made a big impression or whole lifetime patterns that may need to be reviewed to release old hurts and injuries, or clarify your purposes.

Beings can move to other species from life to life, according to their purposes. Some choose to stay in one particular species, such as human or feline, because they like it or find it fulfills their purposes. There are as many reasons and patterns as there are individuals.

6

Dimensions of the Spirit Realm

There are other dimensions, other places,
other games for us to experience.

—Song sparrow

From my many contacts with beings who have departed the physical realm, I am now aware of infinite "places," or dimensions, in the spiritual realm. It's enlightening to experience this wide variety. Beings who have gone on have described to me places of light, places of darkness, places like the Earth (only without the struggle to survive), storybook-like places, meeting with former friends of different species, meetings with angelic beings . . . and much more.

Many animals begin to leave their bodies long before their final breath and start to experience life in the spiritual realm. It's similar to dreaming, with the dream being as real as the physical state.

When we contact beings in the spiritual realm, they may visualize what is real or acceptable to us according to our expectations. It's not unusual for spirits to flash an image of their departed body for recognition, even though they may not actually use that form or image in their existence in another dimension. They may picture themselves to us as young, healthy versions of their former physical self, or they may visualize their spiritual state in various colors and brightness. They sense themselves and each other as spirits in different ways, such as light, as body forms, or as ever-changing. For our benefit, they

71

often picture realms in ways we who are incarnate can relate to or understand.

In the spiritual realm, beings are usually filled with bliss, joy, peace, and connectedness to all. However, if they have issues to complete from life on Earth, they may continue working them out in the spiritual realm and experience a range of emotions as a result. It appears that we reap what we sow, and a great deal of our experience in the spiritual realm seems to be a continuum of what we create in the physical world and vice versa.

Apparently, all realms exist simultaneously and can be glimpsed or experienced in various ways, according to our awareness. Sometimes the spiritual dimensions seem to coexist with the Earth plane, with just a slight veil or difference in vibration separating them. The act of perceiving other realms is like shifting your awareness to lighter forms or tuning in to different television or radio channels. At other times, some beings seem a long "distance" away, in other realms or planes that are not easily accessible for communication. Those who have departed create this distancing according to the "rules" of perceiving or to the purpose of entering a particular realm.

Beings can know each other in the spiritual realm, but they do not seem to be in touch with every other spirit at all times. They go to realms, "departments," or dimensions according to their purposes and visions. It appears that time does not exist, and anything can be created in the spiritual domain. Infinite peace and love are available, although not all beings are able to dwell in this state.

Barbara asked me about her dear horse, Grandpa, who had died a few years before. When I contacted him, he pictured a place that looked like Earth, and he envisioned himself as a horse enjoying himself in a herd of horses. His body was ethereal and light. He suffered no pain or hunger, and he grazed happily in this magical realm.

When I contacted Chester, a rabbit who had recently departed, I was delighted at the realm he showed me. It looked like a storybook, with other spirits in the form of funny creatures that could shift their shape from rabbit-like to anything else. There were many puffy, cloudlike forms resembling trees and houses, but they were all light and malleable.

Maggie, who had passed on a year before as an old dog, said that life in a dog body had its needs, losses, and desperation. Now, she said, there was only total connection and wholeness. She saw her love for her human companion as a continuing circle, unbroken by need or longing. She imaged herself surrounded by light and peace, and she was aware of her former friends and relations who had gone before.

Even if you are unable to contact animals in spirit, you can visualize them in places of peace and beauty. This can help you feel their essence, or even experience visions or sensations from their new realm.

🐾 LESSONS ON THE OTHER SIDE 🐾

There are many lessons to be learned and experiences to enjoy in the spiritual dimensions. Communicator Dawn Baumann Brunke shares glimpses of the other side from her talks with Rooskie, her friend Claire's cat, who died when he was seventeen years old:

On the morning of his journey to the spirit world, Rooskie invited me to "look into death" with him. I saw a bright, blue-purple screen that appeared to be the entrance to a cave. The cave was also filled with soothing blue and purple lights. As I looked into the screen, I saw many images of animals, both living and dying. I understood, then, that the screen could be used to glimpse into the past or future. It was a way for any individual to review "past lives" or consider possible "future lives."

A short time later, Rooskie shared with us that he was taking a rest in the spirit world. He felt it was too early to begin thinking of another life. Instead, he wanted to "drink in the light" of healing and warmth. He was free to assume any form and go anywhere he chose in the spirit world. He noted that time did not exist there in the same way as humans know it.

"I'm here to enjoy the stillness, the sense of presence in the present," Rooskie told us. "I'm just resting and relaxing, and enjoying every moment of 'Now.' You should try this! We could have long talks that would take only seconds in your reality."

About a year after Rooskie left this world, Claire wrote to me and asked, "Is he continuing to have a romp through the dimensions? Will he be coming back? And, if so, when and where, and in what physical form can I find 'him'?"

When I connected with him and asked him Claire's question, Rooskie laughed and said, "Humans always want to know about the future."

He seemed much less connected to his former personality as Rooskie and, curiously, distinctly more female in his (her) presence.

"I am a student right now," Rooskie said. "I'm taking classes in what you might call 'humanhood.' I do have plans to return to Earth, although I haven't yet decided in what form. I am contemplating becoming a human for a short stint of time."

Rooskie gave me the impression she was planning to live on Earth as a young girl, but only to age four or five years, and most likely with a medical condition. Because I was a bit surprised at this, Rooskie began telling me about how some souls, who are new to the human form, come to Earth for just for a short time—to test the waters, so to speak. She told me she was studying about how they might choose to come in as children with disabilities who will die young. Their service to humanity is to help those who want to care for a sick child in order to learn about caring, love, and loss, while the lesson for the soul going in may be about getting a sense of human life, learning about limitations, or simply learning about service to others. Rooskie also noted that some leave early because they have intentionally incarnated into a life form with restrictions (for example, a medical condition), and they want to learn about the bodily form in that way.

Rooskie shared that more knowledge and a deeper sense of understanding are available from the spirit world, which can help humans not to judge these situations based purely on superficial ideas or emotional reactions of pity or sadness. Rooskie pictured her level of learning to me as that of being in grade school. She noted that she needed to take more classes before getting into "college," which was where she wanted to be before her next incarnation.

Rooskie reviewed a number of past lives with me, most of which were in animal form, including a kangaroo, hedgehog, pig (numerous times), goldfish, duck, bear, cat, and dog (both numerous times), as well as a mouse or gerbil who lived with people. Many of her lives as animals were spent with humans, often as a pet or animal companion. Rooskie noted with enthusiasm that she really enjoys humans and is fascinated by the human form. She reasserted that this is why she is in training to do a stint as a human, but for the first few times perhaps only to the child level. She shared that in several past lives as a human she had difficulties with the form, and she felt she needed more study in order to move up to the complexity of the human level.

Rooskie further added that there were special schools for becoming other animals as well. There were even schools for living in different forms on other planets. The whole experience reminded me of a virtual reality scenario—like being on the holodeck, as depicted in the *Star Trek* series. That is, one could choose any form and situation to experience for a short period of time, and these experiences [are] valued highly as a learning device.

Rooskie noted that in her life with Claire she had a high degree of curiosity and a keen desire to learn. She noted that the Rooskie personality she had once "worn" was no longer as present. However, Claire could still tune into the Rooskie she knew, because all forms of Rooskie were still available. Rooskie pictured this to me as a kind of large psychic switchboard. All aspects of Rooskie, in all her various lives and forms, were still available to connect with. All one needed to do was "plug in" to that particular life, with its own unique personality and circumstances, in order to talk and learn more.

Rooskie told me this is how many animals connect to humans in an animal communication session, and it explains why two different people may get two different messages from the same animal. As Rooskie explained it, my level of consciousness is matched with the closest match in her consciousness at the moment we connect. If I had needed simply to talk with Rooskie the cat who once lived with Claire, I could have plugged into that connection. However, it was determined that our conversation (as determined by the connection between Claire, myself, and Rooskie) would be better served by connecting with this larger spirit-being who was once "Rooskie." If my consciousness was such that this connection was too strange, or if the connection would have been damaging to Claire, I simply might not have been able to connect. Instead, I might have been directed to tune into a different version of Rooskie, and a different message (perhaps similar in focus but told in a different way) would have been imparted at that level.

This illustrates the potential of contacting different aspects of animals in spirit. Remember that your own connection is personal and alive in your heart. Your animal friends love you throughout life and death. Your ability to communicate with animal companions after death is a natural continuum of your communication in life.

🐾 PARALLEL EXPERIENCES AFTER DEATH 🐾

To add to the knowledge of the dimensional possibilities after death, and as a contrast to the animal examples in this book, consider the departures of my own parents from this life.

My father called himself an atheist. He never discussed spiritual matters. He was so afraid of dying that in his mid-60s, when his doctor said he would die within a year from high blood pressure unless he stopped drinking, he immediately changed from being a weekend alcoholic to a non-drinker and began pursuing a natural food diet.

He continued to smoke cigars. When he was 80 years old, while fit in every other way, he was diagnosed with lung cancer and died despite having an operation. When I visited him just before his death, I asked him what he thought about the afterlife. Contrary to his previous refusal to talk about spiritual subjects, he talked about how he was going to be with the Hopi Indians when he died. At that time, he was staying with my sister in Arizona near Hopi territory.

Getting close to the time of death tends to make people aware of spiritual realities, even if they have denied them previously. I asked my father what he wanted to do in his next life, and he told me quite lucidly that he wanted to be a Palomino horse. I told him I'd look for him, and he could be my horse if he wanted to. When my visit neared its end, I told him I loved him. For the first time in his life, he was able to say to me, "I love you." It was a beautiful time to be with him. I did not feel grief, but joy that he was at last connecting with his spiritual nature.

In December 1984, my sister called to tell me Dad had departed. When I got in touch with him as a spirit, he was miserable, afraid, and lonely. He pictured himself alone in total darkness. He told me he wanted to be back on Earth and that it was terrible where he was now. I knew he was experiencing what he had created and expected as a spiritual being. I told him there were wonderful beings waiting for him, including his Hopi friends, who would help him if he would turn toward the light and ask. I advised him that it wasn't a good idea to return to Earth until he had fully acknowledged himself as a spiritual being. Otherwise, he would make the same mistakes again. He insisted there was no one there with him, and for several weeks he wallowed in his personal hell of darkness and despair.

When he contacted me again, he was with the Hopi spirits in a medicine circle in the spiritual realm. He was learning from them, and they were taking care of him. Months later, he graduated to a group I call "Alcoholics Anonymous in the Sky," beings who on Earth had the same type of denial of themselves and searched for spirit in a bottle as had my father. In the afterlife, they were helping each other.

Over the years, my father communicated with me every now and then. There were times when he tried to interfere in my life. At other times, he appeared more joyful and whole as a spirit, and he worked with me to resolve incomplete issues from his lives on Earth. Almost twenty years after his death, my father completed his communications with me and his time of evolution in the spiritual realm. Through divine grace, and assisted by prayers and loving communications from me, he moved off the wheel of death and rebirth. He ended his need to reincarnate as an individual identity, and he united completely in a flood of infinite light with the "Source of All."

My mother left the Earth in April 1992. She had smoked cigarettes heavily most of her life and eventually suffered from emphysema and lung cancer. She had been abusive to her children. I did not see her during the last seventeen years of her life because of her negative behavior toward me, which I no longer tolerated. I kept in touch with her telepathically—sending her love and understanding, and conversing on spiritual levels—because contact on the physical plane was too dreadful to bear.

I also kept in touch with her after she left her body and entered the spiritual realm. Unlike my father, my mother believed in a spiritual reality and prayed. She had many issues to work out in the spiritual realm in order to feel at peace. She had a hard time forgiving herself for her own self-hatred and all the harm she had inflicted on her children. She was not in darkness as my father had been, but neither was she enjoying the bliss of being a free spirit.

One day, as I was working on healing the childhood pain and abuse patterns I had incorporated from my parents, I connected with my mother in spirit. I held her in my arms against my heart and danced slowly around the room. I gave her the love she was not able to give me when she was alive. I reviewed her life with her, which revealed and discharged the abuse she had suffered as a child and from my father. I saw how she enacted the same abuse that she had suffered on her own children. She was locked into these ways of being and couldn't act any differently. I felt complete compassion for her and forgave her for all the suffering she had caused me and her other children. In the process of loving her, I felt her soul liberated from the burden of guilt, grief, and pain. She expanded as a spirit, free of all accumulated karmic debt, and peacefully dissolved into the "Infinite Oneness of God."

You can communicate with deceased family members and others (human or nonhuman) even if you are not sure how to do it yet. Start by becoming quiet, closing your eyes, feeling your feet on the ground, and picturing your departed one as he or she appeared in life.

Imagine this person or animal friend is right there with you. Greet them and initiate a conversation. Ask anything you wish, and open your heart to receiving a response. Allow yourself to feel and to express your own feelings. Allow your imagination to guide you. You don't have to be convinced that you are really holding a conversation with a departed family member. Continue to imagine that you are asking questions of your beloved departed one and receiving their answers. You may not get all your questions answered in one session. Applaud yourself for making contact or at least imagining that you could. You may wish to write down what happened during your communication session. Let yourself assimilate your experience. If you wish, make contact and communicate with your human or animal friend in spirit another time.

7

Guilt and Grieving

When animals enter our life, we start on a journey filled with
adventure, learning, and love. The animals reach deep into us and
change us in ways that can hardly be described. We grow in love. And
upon their leaving, we are lost, devastated. Over time, we explore the
story and see the meaning, and stand in awe of these remarkable
beings. What an honor they give us when they walk
a part of our lives with us.

—Barbara Janelle

When our beloved animal friends depart this world, whatever the
circumstances, we often feel gut-wrenching emotions over the loss.
Anger, sadness, guilt, fear, and denial may hold us in their grip. It's
natural to feel devastated when we lose the presence of the animal
friends who bring us so much joy, love, pleasure, and even enlighten-
ment. Cathy Malkin-Currea relates her experience:

When my beloved dog, Kite Chaser (KC the Keeshond), suddenly
became ill and died in January 2002, I gained a deeper understanding of
the dying process and the insidious nature of grief. I still grieve for KC's
physical presence, but I now know that the depth of my grief is a reflection of the depth of love I have for him.

To find relief and eventually peace, we have to face, accept, and
express the darker feelings, along with the happiness we have shared

with our beloved animal companions. Writing a memorial poem or
story, or doing a work of art or a photo collage in their memory and
sending it to others who have also loved your animal companion can
help you to honor, move through, and release your loss. Having a ceremony or a party with friends, joining a support group, or going for grief
counseling can all be part of honoring your animal companion and
your feelings, and learning to accept death as part of the cycle of life.

Sometimes the guilt and grief can be pervasive and seem impossible to
move through. Sharon Callahan expresses the depth of how animals
can touch our hearts:

> It's always difficult to lose someone we love, but the death of an animal
> companion often touches us even more profoundly than the death of a
> human being. Our animal friends at times grow dearer to us than our
> closest human friends. They love us so unconditionally and with such
> great presence that their passing can leave a profound emptiness in the
> deepest recesses of our heart and soul.
>
> Because most companion animals perform their self-appointed tasks
> of teaching us about unconditional love and surrender so magnificently,
> we often experience with them what we have only dreamed of with our
> human loved ones. When the animal dies, there is a natural tendency, in
> addition to the grief we experience over their passing, to also feel grief
> about not feeling loved in the same way by the humans in our lives. We
> may also experience an outpouring of emotion we would like to be able
> to express to our human lovers and friends, but feel we cannot. Then our
> bereavement tends to evolve into nonspecific grief over the lack of love
> we witness in the world in general, the absence of which is made all the
> more noticeable by the absence of our four-legged friends.
>
> Our society as a whole denies death. Youth is worshiped, old folks are
> whisked off to "the home," and the topic of death is avoided by almost
> everyone. The witnessing of the full spectrum of an animal's life brings us

face to face with our own mortality and is often the most intimate glimpse of illness, aging, and death that we may ever get.

When an animal dies, we often experience feelings of remorse that compound our grief further. Could I have done more for my beloved companion? Why was I so preoccupied with my work that I failed to notice his illness? Did the treatment plan I chose cause him to suffer more? These questions and many others may haunt us for weeks, months, or possibly years.

Our rational minds may tell us it isn't logical to grieve so much for an animal companion. However, every bond we share with another being creates a kind of energetic blending of our auras, or energy fields. There is a tearing of this bond when a friend leaves, which can feel like our bodies are being ripped open. We have to heal this energetic wound before we can easily connect with our friend in spirit.

🐾 ANIMAL PEACE, HUMAN GUILT 🐾

We don't know everything there is to know about the cycle of life and death. It seems to be part of human nature, or at least our cultural conditioning, to blame ourselves or feel guilty about the death of our animal companions. This assumes that we are in control, or should be in control, of another being's life and death, or be able to prevent death.

Travis and Carmen had the disastrous experience of having their home burn to the ground, resulting in the loss of some members of their animal family. The most painful loss was the death of their young Siamese cat, Faith. In his attempt to save the horses and chickens while the fire raged, Travis had pushed over a heavy outdoor bench. When Travis and Carmen returned after the fire was over to see if they could find more of the animals, Travis found Faith dead under the bench. He thought he had killed her and couldn't forgive himself. Weeks later, he consulted me about it.

Contacting Faith was an incredible experience. She had positioned herself over the charred property as a shining, huge spirit and created a large energy field to help the trees and other plants grow. Carmen commented that she and the neighbors, whose properties were also scorched, were amazed that the trees and plants on Carmen's property were already sprouting new shoots, while the neighbors' trees showed no sign of life. Faith said that when her job of restoring the land was done and the house had been rebuilt, she would return to her human family as a Siamese cat. She told me her death was not directly caused by Travis. She was in shock and suffering from the smoke and fire, so she hid under the bench. The blow from the bench helped her to leave her body suddenly instead of slowly. She held no bad feelings from the incident.

Faith's story illustrates that finding out how animals feel after death can greatly assist the whole process of coming to terms with our feelings and finding peace.

🐾 ANIMAL SADNESS COMPOUNDING GRIEF 🐾

Sometimes, the grief and guilt we feel is compounded by the animal's sadness at not being able to have the kind of death and timing they needed to feel complete with their lives. Professional counseling and help communicating with the departed animal might be needed to relieve the emotional pain.

Tanya called me because she felt awful about her dog Suki's recent euthanasia. Twelve-year-old Suki had cancer in her nose, and the vets advised that she be put down. Tanya felt that Suki didn't want to go, but Tanya was desperate. When I contacted Suki, she was sad and still hanging around Tanya. She had wanted two more weeks to complete her life emotionally, and she felt she had been wrenched from her body.

Suki experienced relief as she communicated with me. At first, she felt she couldn't move on until she had been around for a few weeks to complete her life with Tanya. As Tanya listened and understood Suki's communication, I saw Suki spiritually transformed into a beautiful blue light that turned white, like brilliant sunbeams, as she lifted to another dimension. Her transition was complete. She had become Tanya's angel guardian. Tanya wrote to me about her experience:

When I hung up the phone after talking with you, I went into a room with sunbeams, where she used to bask during the day. The sun shines in through a skylight, and as I gazed into the sky, just trying to be with her, a huge cloud formed itself into the image of her face. Where her ears should have been, were huge, fluffy wings, and surrounding her were many other indiscernible beings. The cloud dissipated within a few minutes. Whether I was just seeing things or not, I felt her and cried and cried. I could let her go, finally, and it did feel free and loving, loving, loving.

Nancy had been distraught over euthanizing Sarah, her mother's cat, two days before, and she contacted animal communicator Tricia Hart for help.

Nancy cared for her sick mother during her final days, and Sarah was more than Nancy felt she could handle during the trying time of losing her mother. When Sarah got sick and the vet suggested euthanasia, Nancy decided it was the best option. Nancy later worried that she had Sarah euthanized before the cat was ready.

I contacted Sarah and asked her how she was doing, and how she felt about being euthanized. Sarah expressed her surprise and confusion upon finding herself on the other side. She had not been ready to go and, at first, she had no idea what had happened. Sarah showed me an image of herself waking up, looking around, shaking her head with wide eyes, and trying to discern where she was.

Sarah felt a little remorse that she had not been there for Helen (Nancy's mother) during her transition, which is one of the reasons Sarah wanted to stay on Earth. Sarah quickly mentioned that Nancy should be told she was fine. Sarah had adjusted to her situation and was happy to help Helen from the spiritual dimension. Sarah did not want

Nancy to feel bad about what had happened. The decision had been made, the injection was administered, and there was no reason to spend any time feeling bad about what could not be changed.

Nancy seemed to get some relief from Sarah's communications. Although the burden of losing her mother was heavy, letting go of the worry about Sarah helped her cope.

Even when animals find some aspect of their death confusing or surprising, they generally love to connect with their human companion and are completely understanding and forgiving of any details surrounding their departure. Knowing this can help you release any guilt about not doing something "right" in your animal friend's dying process.

🐾 HUMAN GRIEF HOLDING BACK AN ANIMAL 🐾

Sometimes human grief and attachment to having the animal in the physical body may prevent an animal who has already departed from being completely free in the spiritual realm.

Mary Ann contacted animal communicator Catherine Ferguson for grief counseling after the death of Ginger, her golden retriever. Catherine explains the experience:

I found that Ginger wasn't integrating into her new surroundings in the spiritual realm because Mary Ann's grief was holding her back. We discussed various ways that Mary Ann could honor Ginger's life and lay her to rest.

After the second session, I learned that Ginger was adjusting to her new life in spirit and was being groomed to become a spirit therapy dog for young children confined to hospitals. She was sure she would enjoy the work. Mary Ann was still sad for her loss, but she was happy to see that her efforts to release Ginger were paying off.

A few days later, Ginger came to me in a dream. She was doing a slow, deliberate dance, standing on her hind legs, stepping one or two steps to the right, then back to the left. She kept time by snapping her front toes as if they were fingers. She had a good dancing style and a good sense of rhythm. I understood the message for Mary Ann was that Ginger was doing well, regaining her strength, and enjoying herself. Mary Ann told me that she and her husband frequently danced with Ginger, so the dog was obviously acknowledging a shared activity and showing that she hadn't forgotten how to dance.

Mary Ann didn't need any more sessions with me, and a few months later she was able to bring a new puppy into her life.

From this, we learn how important it is to move through your own grief process and get whatever help you need, both for your sake and to help your animal friend move on.

🐾 MOVING THROUGH THE GRIEF 🐾

There are many ways we can help ourselves heal from the loss of our animal friends. Barbara Janelle addresses her clients' grief with a process that gives people a chance to speak about their animals, explore their stories, and recognize the awesome gifts the animals offered. Try this for yourself, either speaking to a friend or writing down the answers:

🐾 State the animal's name and give a physical description.

🐾 Briefly tell how the animal died.

🐾 How did this animal come to you? You may recognize that the animal's coming was no accident and that the animal was meant to appear at the time and in the way he or she did.

🐾 Tell about something the animal did that made you laugh.

🐾 Was there something the animal did that annoyed you?

🐾 What adventures did you have together?

🐾 What part of your life did the animal walk with you?

🐾 What did the animal teach you?

🐾 Describe in single words or short phrases your animal's character. Put "I am" in front of each of those descriptions. You may see how the animal mirrored so much for you.

🐾 Invite the animal to come into your mind and heart. See the animal before you.

🐾 Tell the animal whatever you want him or her to know. Thank the animal.

🐾 Receive whatever the animal gives in return.

🐾 Later, go out and look at the evening sky. Quite often one star stands out and the feeling of the animal's generous spirit is present.

COMING TO TERMS WITH ANIMAL DEATH—THE ANIMALS' VIEW

Kate was extremely upset when she communicated to me about a friend's husky wolf mix, Roy, who had killed her cat, Sheila. It happened while Kate was taking care of the dog in her home. Kate played with Roy and then went inside to clean the house. When she went out again to check on Roy, she found him trying to get Sheila, who was clawing at him on top of a pile of boards. Kate couldn't get Roy to leave so she grabbed her cat by the scruff of the neck. Roy grabbed Sheila by the belly and pulled her out of Kate's hands, shaking the cat until she was lifeless. Kate threw things at Roy to try and stop him, but she only succeeded in getting the cat away from Roy when she kicked at him. By then it was too late. She felt the dog had intended to eat the cat's body.

Kate was miserable and asked me to tell Sheila she was sorry. She wanted me to tell Roy that what he did was wrong, and now he could not visit her because of her other cats.

Your animal friends can receive your communications without someone else repeating what you want to say, but you may feel so distraught that you are unable to communicate or receive well. Therefore, it can be helpful to have a neutral party assist you. When I checked in with Sheila, she had this message for Kate:

Dearest friend,

Know that I am at peace. I am in a beautiful space of oneness. In this realm, the birds sing cheerfully, the sky is blue, the sun is warm, the air is fresh and full of good smells, and everything is so peaceful. There are other cat spirits here, and dogs, other large and small animals, and plenty of humans. We are all transparent to each other. That is, we can see through and be with each other in any way we wish. There is no danger, pain, frustration, or misunderstanding. It is indeed heaven—what Earth would be like at its best, in pure harmony with all beings.

There is nothing you could have done to prevent this transition of my spirit from physical form to the spirit realm. Roy and I locked into each other when I first saw him. We were magnetically attracted to each other, and we both knew there was something we were meant to accomplish together. At first, it was scary when you tried to rescue me and he grabbed my body, but instantly I was catapulted out of my body and felt a sense of joy and freedom I had never known. I watched the scene from afar. It was like watching a movie from the sky, only with eagle-eye vision. I knew that I had been given a great gift, because now I would not die a slow death as my body decayed. I was swiftly moved to the place where I belong as a spirit in perfect peace.

I'm sorry you suffered and blamed yourself for my death, but I was meant to leave. I don't want you to misunderstand the motives and actions of Roy and me. It was our pact, our doing. Don't think of him as a bad dog. He was doing what came naturally for him and in relationship to me. I also aroused his hunting instinct by my actions. It was all perfectly orchestrated for a swift transfer. Please understand. It was exciting for him. I made it so by my nature as a cat and my actions. I was meant to be part of him and he part of me. Now we are totally one. We understand and feel this on the deepest spirit level.

I wish you acceptance that brings peace, instead of misunderstanding that brings suffering. I love you and appreciate the great life in the sun we had together on Earth. It all seems so perfect to me now. I see exactly how and why I lived, and the perfection of returning to my spirit home. All is well. Let it be so with you. I wish you the peace that I feel now.

I also checked with Roy about the incident. He felt Kate's hurt and anger toward him, and was sad that she was upset. He felt deep inside that his nature was to live with people according to their pack rules, but he also experienced the instinct to hunt, as was natural to his breeding. Roy normally did not express the urge to hunt and kill other animals because his life was generally structured by humans and this was not aroused. However, he felt excited and focused with Sheila in the hunting game. There was such a strong energy propelling him to grab and kill the cat, and to become one with her by ingesting her body. He also felt on a deep level that he was meant to play this part with her. Roy was sorry Kate was so hurt, and had accepted that Kate did not want him around her cats, feeling that his action was very wrong for her. He wasn't sure if anything like that would happen again with other cats; it all happened so quickly for Roy and could not be undone. I experienced Roy as a loving, lively, and intelligent dog. He was not malicious in his intent. Just as he and Sheila had said, he was following their united action and intentions.

This example and the next show us that no matter how much we want everything to be "perfect" for our animal friends, they sometimes plan their lives and deaths in surprising ways that may be contrary to what we want for them. Some things are beyond our control.

Toni bottle-fed her cat Michaela from the time she was a few days old and saved her life. This led to a tremendous bond between the two of them. However, their time together on Earth lasted only a couple of years, until Michaela's traumatic death. Despite the years that had passed since Michaela's death, counseling, and working with her grief and the guilt she felt about how Michaela had died, Toni was having great difficulty dealing with the loss. Her counselor felt that communication with Michaela might bring Toni the relief she sought. Toni called animal communicator Sondy Kaska for help. Sondy tells about her consultation with Michaela and Toni:

Michaela came barging into my consciousness. She appeared as a petite, black- and white-spotted kitty with boundless energy. She demanded to know, "What's taking her [Toni] so long?" Michaela wanted Toni to heal and to know she was not upset with Toni about her death. She said to tell Toni she did nothing wrong.

Michaela said she came to Toni to help her grow and to open her heart. Michaela said she taught Toni to laugh again, and commented that she will be back, maybe in a different form.

"I might try another form. I love adventure!" Michaela said. Toni confirmed that little Michaela had always been adventurous.

Michaela showed me where she was in the spiritual realm. It was peaceful, with lots of sunshine in a meadow filled with flowers and butterflies. Michaela said she loved the sunshine and could never get enough of it on Earth.

Toni told Michaela how intensely she loved and missed her. It was important to Toni that Michaela know she had a tremendous amount of gratitude for what Michaela had taught her about love. Michaela said she already knew and that she was right there with Toni all the time.

Michaela said, "Mom, don't you feel me?" Toni didn't, but Michaela was there, watching over her. Michaela said that Toni needed to let her go. Toni's feelings of guilt about Michaela's death were overwhelming. I asked her what had happened.

Toni had been moving. She thought that Michaela was safely locked in the bathroom, so she had propped the front door open while some bigger pieces of furniture were being moved out of the house. However, the bathroom door did not close tightly, and Michaela was able to pry it open. She got out of the bathroom and then darted out through the open door.

Two neighborhood dogs had escaped from their yard and ventured into Toni's yard. Toni ran to Michaela's aid and tried to fend off the dogs, but they were in a frenzy and attacked Toni. She was able to pull Michaela away, but the dogs got her again and that was the end.

Toni always felt she had made a mistake by not running indoors the instant she grabbed Michaela away, but instead she put the cat on top of the fence post while she tried to get the dogs out of the yard. Toni felt she had lost her chance to save Michaela and had failed her dear cat.

Michaela's view was that Toni did nothing wrong and that what happened was not her fault. I asked what else Michaela had to say about her death.

"I didn't know fear, and I was going to teach Mom not to be afraid, but this wasn't a good example of how to do it," she replied.

Michaela continued, "I know she feels bad, but it wasn't her fault. It was my time to go. She's never going to heal unless she quits blaming herself."

Michaela also showed me that when the dogs attacked for the last time, her spirit left her body and she escaped the pain of the attack. One minute Michaela was in her body, and the next moment she was gone. Toni always wondered why—if Michaela was still alive when she put her on the fence post—she didn't jump down and run to safety. Michaela responded that it was her time to go. Toni said that at the time of her cat's death, she saw something she could only describe as a swooping bird.

Toni said Michaela had opened her up to more joy than she had ever known, and Michaela reminded her that joy is always available. Michaela did not wait for anything to happen or wish for things to be different. She had experienced joy in the world each day with the sunshine, a butterfly to chase, grass to roll in, and in everything she did.

I asked Michaela why she chose to leave at the time she did.

"You cannot really know joy until you know the biggest sorrow," she said. "I taught Toni all I could about joy without showing her the sorrow. My mission, my job in life is to teach people this. I did it for Toni, and now I have to teach others.

Michaela continued, "I know our bond was deeper and more special than anything Toni had ever experienced. My love with my mom needs to be a door for her that opens wide. Because she has so much love in her heart now, she needs to be able to give love to lots of other beings."

Toni said one of the reasons she had not tried to contact Michaela sooner was because she was afraid that Michaela was angry with her. Toni realized she had been so wrapped up in her guilt and blame that it prevented her from recognizing when Michaela's spirit was around and still teaching her. Toni knew she needed to release her guilt and blame, but she never felt she had Michaela's permission to forgive herself. Now she was reassured that Michaela wanted her to forgive herself and move on in order to spread the joy she learned from her beloved little feline.

Michaela ended our session by singing a little song, "Michaela, Michaela, I'll always be your Michaela," just like Toni had always sung to her!

🐾 WE CANNOT CONTROL DEATH 🐾

I learned a graphic lesson about the nature of death from several duck members of our family, and how we may be contributing agents, but we are not usually in control of another's departure. I'll relay the story in detail, because it illustrates many aspects of the cycle of life and death.

My first ducklings were two males named Maximilian and Marigold. As they grew, Marigold became aloof, and one day announced that he didn't want to live here and was going away. I simply acknowledged him, as he did not wish to talk further about it. A week later, Marigold was killed by raccoons. Then I understood that he had decided to leave his body and dwell elsewhere.

Our female Afghan hound, Rana, was a wonderful guardian of the chickens, ducks, and other animals in the family. She kept predators away with great skill and consistency. Rana was embarrassed when I told her the raccoons had killed Marigold during the night. She could hardly believe it. I explained that Marigold had wanted to leave and it was his own choice, but Rana took her job seriously. The next night she stayed on guard near Maximilian and barked at the approach of any wild critter.

Maximilian and I became closer friends after Marigold's death. However, when he tried to mate with me, I decided he needed a female duck companion! It was love at first sight when Marimba, an adult female duck, arrived. Not only did Maximilian vigorously mate with her, but he caressed and loved her with great devotion.

Maximilian defended Marimba from any other animal that approached. He particularly directed his attacks at Rana. He would lunge and bite at her, even when she was peacefully sleeping. I counseled him not to do this because Rana did not deserve to be attacked. Rana, in fact, was the defender of ducks. Maximilian did not listen. Rana tolerated his attacks and tried to avoid being around him rather than striking back. However, Rana was always startled by Maximilian, and we found later that she resented his blows.

One weekend, my former husband and I were out of town and had house-sitters taking care of things. When we returned at night, Maximilian did not call to us as usual and was nowhere to be found. I did not question everyone then, but I noticed that Rana was a bit quiet. The next morning, I found Maximilian's body in the yard, his neck broken and torn. Rana must have had enough of Maximilian's attacks and had struck back. We were all devastated. Maximilian had been special to all of us as the shining, personable communicator he was.

For several days, Marimba cried long honks of grief for Maximilian. Rana felt sick about what she had done and would not eat. We missed him terribly. When I contacted Maximilian, he was angry. He wanted to be back with Marimba and resented his life being cut short. It was December and not the time for baby ducks, so he could not reincarnate in the same species to be back with us right away. He hung around spiritually to look after Marimba, but Marimba was lonely just the same.

I decided to find an adult male duck to keep Marimba company until Maximilian could come back, if by spring duckling season he still chose to do so. I had noticed some domesticated ducks living together on a nearby stream. I went to them and explained that I needed a male companion for Marimba.

A male duck I was interested in came forward to get close to me, but another male shouted to him, "Danger, she's going to grab you, watch it." My chosen male got frightened and hurried back to the stream with the others. I told him I'd be back the next day with a cage to take him home if he wanted to come with me. The next day, he came forward willingly and was docile when I put him in the cage. On the way home, he told me he wanted to be called Geronimo.

Marimba was not impressed with Geronimo. Her first comment was that he wasn't Maximilian. It was weeks before she allowed him to mate with her, but gradually they became good friends. Maximilian was now planning to return as one of Marimba's ducklings in the spring. Marimba went to nest, but when she left her nest briefly each day to eat and bathe, our dogs always managed to find out where she was nesting and eat her eggs. She refused to nest in a caged area the dogs could not reach, so her attempts to have ducklings were unsuccessful.

The year went by, and Maximilian kept in touch but did not return. That winter, Geronimo became restless. He had changed from a timid fellow to an aggressive one who attacked people, dogs, cats, or whoever came near. Geronimo was not happy. He wanted to go back to his wild life on the stream.

One day, he insisted that I take him back, along with Marimba. When I asked Marimba if she wanted to go or stay with us, she said she was afraid of going to the stream and wanted to stay. Geronimo then did something I had never seen him do, but which reminded me of how Maximilian had been with Marimba. He nuzzled Marimba all over her neck and face, and said he wanted her to go with him. She agreed.

I waited until the next day, which was perfect weather for their release. It was raining, so I thought there wouldn't be people walking their dogs near the stream like they did in fair weather. When we took Geronimo and Marimba to a place along the stream where Geronimo had often been, it was raining hard and no one else was around. Perfect, I thought. Marimba will have a peaceful time to get used to being in the wild.

Geronimo waddled into the familiar, deep and wide creek with great joy, quickly swimming to the middle. Marimba was hesitant, but she followed him. They were in the stream about one minute when the unbelievable happened. A black Labrador dog suddenly appeared, raced toward the stream, and leaped in after the ducks. I was horrified and stood helplessly on the shore. Marimba and Geronimo were heavy, domestic ducks, not suited for flying. Marimba flapped and dove for the high weeds on the far shore. She disappeared as the dog swam after her. The dog then chased Geronimo, but he flapped and swam fast downstream, and the dog gave up after about a quarter of a mile.

I looked for Marimba, but I intuitively knew what had happened. The shock and exertion of being chased had killed her almost instantly, as if her heart had burst. The stream was too wide and deep for us to get to the other side, and we never found her body. After the dog was taken away, Geronimo came back, looking for Marimba. He quacked repeatedly for her, but she did not answer. After awhile, he knew she was gone and returned downstream, where the other small group of domestic ducks he already knew usually gathered.

I went home feeling I had killed Marimba. After all, she hadn't really wanted to go, but Geronimo had convinced her, or had he? I went back an hour later to look again for Marimba, just in case I had been in error about her death. When I returned to the spot, I received a message that totally shifted my awareness of this whole incident.

I tried to contact Marimba to verify what had happened and see how she was doing. Instead, Maximilian came in and said, "Do you really think you are in control of someone else's fate? I called Marimba to be with me. We were meant to be together, and her time had come. In the garden, when you asked if she wanted to go with Geronimo to the stream, I acted through Geronimo and nuzzled her and encouraged her to come, knowing she would be released from her body to be with me."

I became aware of Marimba as a spirit near Maximilian, still a bit shocked by the whole affair, but happy that she was with Maximilian. He told me he would take care of her and that now he did not need to come back to Earth.

I felt humbled, filled with the realization that when the time to depart the body comes, there is little or nothing someone else can do about it. One way or another, it will happen. While I was apparently the agent of Marimba's death or, at least, assisted in the circumstances, I was *not* the cause. I had no intention of killing her and was simply doing what I thought she wanted. I saw now that Maximilian had arranged it, and Marimba had agreed because of their desire to be together.

🐾 FINDING JOY AGAIN 🐾

It might seem impossible, when we are wrapped in the throes of grief and loss after an animal departs, but we can find joy again. So much depends on communicating and really feeling the eternal connection with our animal friends.

A client named Roanna had experienced much pain and guilt from the loss of her rabbit, Thumper, a few years prior to consulting with me about it. After I contacted Thumper, Roanna wrote to me:

To my delight, Thumper was taking care of lots of bunnies in a beautiful place with rolling hills, green grass, sweet-smelling air, sunshine, and flowers. The reason Thumper gave for having "checked out" was something that only she and I would know, spoken from her viewpoint: "It was really quiet for a long time, and I wanted to be around lots of bunnies," Thumper said. "Even if I had babies I wouldn't let you get rid of them."

Interestingly, my boyfriend and I had discussed allowing Bogie and Thumper to have one litter before Bogie was neutered, but we decided not to because I would not have been able to let anyone take the babies without lifelong visitation rights. My attitude towards death changed completely after this communication from Thumper.

Through consultations and rediscovering her own telepathic abilities, Roanna kept in touch with Larissa, another rabbit friend, while

Larissa was dying of cancer. She then wrote, "Participating in Larissa's death has been one of the most wonderful experiences of my life. In death there is joy."

When Chico San, my angora, calico cat, did not come home one day, which was not her habit, we were concerned. I felt she was okay, but as the days went by, I thought she might be dead. Whenever I contacted her, I got that she was in the woods relaxing and hunting, and that she needed this time alone. After about four days, I experienced a vision of her body lying on the forest floor and her spirit ascending with white, golden light, like an angel. Her body seemed asleep. However, when she started assisting me in long-distance healings by adding powerful spiritual energy, I thought she must have died.

In tribute to Chico San at what seemed to be the end of her life on Earth, I made a collage of photos taken of her and hung it in my office. I found peace and joy in celebrating our life together, even though it seemed strange to think she might never walk through the door again.

One morning a week later, Chico San appeared, none the worse for wear except for a few ticks and fleas. She told me she had been on a kind of sabbatical or vision quest for her spiritual advancement. I understood but was so glad to have her back.

ANIMAL GRIEVING

Animals also grieve for the loss of loved ones and may need help in releasing their grief and finding peace. As the following experience shows, ritual can help them, too.

Animal communicator Karen Craft met Caesar, an English bulldog, at a pet store grand opening. He was exuberant because it was his birthday, and his human friends, Robin and Joe, were celebrating by bringing him to talk with Karen and letting him pick out some treats.

A few months later, Robin telephoned to tell Karen that Caesar was despondent and constantly whimpering since the death of her father. Robin tells the story:

My dad died on March 25, 2004. Almost immediately, Caesar changed from being the happy, seemingly carefree puppy we had always known and loved to a nervous wreck who cried all the time. He seemed miserable. He started staying in bed until noon; this little guy had previously always made sure we were out of bed no later than 7:30. We knew something was wrong, and our vet confirmed that he was probably depressed over the passing of my father. My dad had stayed with us for three months just prior to his death. He left our house and died one week later. Caesar had been Dad's companion all through an illness we thought had been corrected successfully through surgery. Dad and Caesar had been long-standing pals for years. We just didn't know what to do for the little guy.

In July, my family came to our house for a group journey to Wyoming to scatter my dad's ashes. Just after this, Caesar became more agitated than ever. One day I came home for lunch and Caesar ran up to me and started barking in my face. We knew we had to do something. We remembered meeting Karen at the pet store the previous November, so we called her.

Karen told us Caesar was indeed depressed over Dad's passing. He felt he was the caregiver in charge of Dad's health and that he'd failed him, especially since he wasn't with Grandpa when he passed. He also felt sad that he hadn't been able to say good-bye.

Caesar had become more agitated after my family's visit. He could see we had gotten closure. We comforted each other, but no one was comforting him. He was also agitated because my father had given him a message for me.

Karen suggested we conduct a ceremony for my dad. She said Caesar needed the closure, and we needed it as well. Karen also recommended we do one or more smudges (use of burning herbs for purification) after our ceremony.

Then Karen told us she had Caesar's message from my dad, but it didn't really make sense. She said my dad told Caesar to tell us that he apologized. As soon as Karen said that the hair on my husband's and my neck stood on end. It made perfect sense to us. We used to chastise Dad for apologizing all the time, often when he had not even contributed to the problem.

So we planned our ceremony. We gathered a ton of my Dad's possessions and piled them on the floor. We lit a red candle (Dad's favorite color), and brought out the poetry we had used at the ceremony in Wyoming. Then we called the dogs in. Brutus came first and sat next to Joe and me. Caesar came in and climbed on top of the pile of my Dad's stuff (very uncharacteristic of him) and sat there. I explained to the dogs that we were gathered to say goodbye to Grandpa and the ceremony was to bring closure for all of us. Then we read the poetry and talked some more. As soon as we had concluded the ceremony, Caesar stood up, picked up one of my Dad's baseball caps, and started to shred it. Half-heartedly, I tried to take it away from him, but he grabbed it and ran across the room. He ripped the cap into pieces somewhat violently, which was not like him.

When he finished shredding, he picked up the whole mess, walked over to me and placed it in my lap. Then he lay down next to the pile of my dad's stuff and stayed there for about ten minutes. After awhile, I went over and lay down about a foot away from him. He got up and walked over to me; we sat together for a few minutes and then he walked away and sat with his back to me. That's when I knew the ceremony was really over.

Caesar improved a little, immediately after the ceremony. After the first smudge he improved more, and after the second smudge (a month later) he was back to being our same carefree guy. It was exactly as Karen had said.

Karen had been a bit nervous about suggesting to Robin and Joe that they hold a private funeral service for their dogs to attend. But they liked the idea and lovingly carried it out. Caesar knew just how to express his frustration over not having the chance to say good-bye to his beloved grandpa and then being unable to attend the formal funeral—as if he weren't part of the family! His human family had given him a beautiful, sensitive opportunity to do his emotional healing.

🐾 WHALE ADVICE ON HANDLING DEATH 🐾

Not only do we have to contend with the emotions that come with our animal companions' deaths, but strong feelings, including help-lessness, anger, sorrow, and revenge may surge when we witness or hear about the death of wild animals, especially those caused by human actions. Animal communicator Teresa Wagner received counsel from the great whales on how to work with this.

The day was exceptionally warm for early October on the waters off of Provincetown, Massachusetts. Sitting on the bow of the boat, feeling the warm, gentle breezes touch my skin and hair, I was delighted to need only a T-shirt and shorts to go whale watching in the Gulf of Maine. I had been traveling here for many years to see humpback whales during the spring and fall weather, but this was the first time it was so warm out on the water. Little did I know that soon I would be stunned by a bigger surprise and offered one of the most important lessons of my life.

As we made our journey offshore to the humpback feeding grounds of Stellwagon Bank, passing the long, sandy shoreline of the Province-town peninsula, I was in great spirits. It was a long weekend; I was in the company of good friends; and I felt the joyful anticipation of soon seeing humpbacks—my family, my elders, my teachers and guides whom I love beyond measure.

Suddenly, I heard one of my friends standing at the railing say, "Oh God, don't let Teresa see this." Everyone was moving to the side of the boat facing the shoreline. I felt dread inside. I knew something was wrong involving a whale. I moved to the side of the boat and saw the dead baby humpback lying on the beach, and the dorsal fins and spouts of two adults swimming nearby. My heart broke seeing the exquisite, young humpback's body, out of her water element and lying lifeless on the edge of land where she didn't belong. The on-board scientist began to speak about the research that would be done to determine possible causes of this death. She cited statistics about collisions with boats and boat motors, entanglements with fishing nets, and toxins in the water as common causes of injury, disease, and death of whales in this area and around the world.

As I listened, I felt a wretched rip of grief in my heart like fire. Although I was already well aware of the many human-caused deaths of whales, hearing it again while actually looking at this beautiful, dead whale child, consumed me with anger toward the humans who every day directly and indirectly cause the death of whales for profit or science. I was angry, heartbroken, and inconsolable.

I went to a far corner of the boat to be alone, telling my friends I needed some quiet time. Just when I thought I might never overcome my struggle to come to peace, I heard a familiar beloved voice.

"I am here to hold and support your heart, and to help you see how to better serve the whales you love. You've taken a wrong turn here, and I will help you find your way back. It's time for you to learn an extremely important lesson, one that will decrease your own pain of outrage and grief, and also help the whale who has died and all those who love her."

It was the voice of the first whale I had ever seen in this life, a soul with whom I had a long history and who supports me as a father and wise guide. Sometimes, I get lazy and don't listen or act on the intuitive messages and help I receive. But when he speaks to me, I always listen. He continued.

"I am going to help you channel the overwhelming, natural energy of your grief into powerful support for the one who has died, for her loved ones, those who may have harmed her, and yourself. This is what I want you to do:

"First, take a deep breath, steady yourself, and fill yourself with love. Get back in touch with that wellspring of love within you that you know is limitless and ever present. Allow your soul to support your broken heart. Fill your heart and every cell in your body, and every space in your energy field, with great love. Gently, completely. Remember the being of love that you are. From this centered place of your soul, which knows peace even in the midst of chaos and pain, remember this: you are never helpless to shower someone who is suffering with great love, even when you cannot help on the physical plane.

"Second, send this great love to the soul of the whale who has died. Send love with peace and gentleness, yet with great power and intention from the depth of your soul. Surround the soul of the whale with all the love of the universe. Thank her for having graced the Earth with her presence. Ask for blessings for the journey of her soul through all time and space. Bow to her in awe and gratitude for all she was and is.

"Third, send this same great love, and also comfort, to the loved ones of the whale. As much as you hurt, they are the primary grievers of this loss, and they hurt even more. It's important to tend to them before yourself. Surround them with great depths of love and the energy of soft, nurturing comfort and compassion. Let them know they are not alone in their grief—that you, too, care deeply about their great loss.

"Fourth, send the same great love and deep compassion now to those you believe may have caused the death of this whale and others—those you see as the perpetrators. This is where you took a wrong turn earlier. You became stuck when you went directly into anger at those who caused the suffering, rather than going first to love. Now, send the same limitless love to those known and unknown to you who created this death, to those who are not yet able to see and act from their hearts, and to those who are not yet conscious enough to see the souls of animals. Send them love, for it's only with compassion and love that their consciousness will expand and their hearts will understand. Send them compassion, because at one time you, too, were not as conscious as you are today, and it was from the compassion of others that you grew.

"Finally, express and tend to your own grief and pain. Do what you must to express your own grief and anger. Honor your feelings, however deep, dark, confusing, or contradictory they may be. Ask for help from beings you trust, on Earth and in spirit, to help you understand and fully release your pain.

"Do not expect the one who died or her loved ones to support you. They are the primary grievers and need your support. You are a secondary griever and need support from others. There is always enough love and support for everyone. It's important to discern when and where to turn for help.

"Now is the time for you to take care of yourself. Reach out for help from your own soul and from earthly and spiritual beings who will understand. Your own heart and pain is as important as the suffering of the whales. Tend to yourself now with great compassion and love."

I followed his suggestions as he spoke them. Remarkably, by the time I completed the second step, my own anger and grief was tremendously lessened. By the time I got to the step of asking for and receiving help for my own heart, hardly any help was needed because I was so filled with the grace of meeting these souls with love.

I still get angry with people who harm animals. I still grieve deeply when animals die. But now I consciously respond and process my feelings in a different way and in a different order. This allows me to better serve the animals I love so much, and allows my own suffering to move to quiet acceptance and peace much sooner.

I use this process when I see animals on the side of the road, obviously killed by a human's vehicle. I used to feel greatly overwhelmed by grief. I was angry at speeding drivers and the humans who have allowed animal habitat to be turned into highways. Now, using this process, I no longer feel overwhelmed and alienated. I am part of the healing of all beings. My level of compassion has matured. My ability to help has increased, and I am grateful.

This process is not about ignoring one's own grief—it's about dealing with it after first offering love and compassion to those directly impacted.

The process is not about pretending suffering does not exist, that people on Earth do not harm animals, or condoning what they do. It's about showering those who create suffering with love, rather than adding the energy of anger and hatred to souls already unconscious about animals.

The process is not about sending love instead of practical help. It's about sending love in addition to any political action, rescue efforts, or donations you might choose to make.

My whale father described it best when he told me it's about channeling our overwhelming, natural energy of grief and anger in response to harm into powerful support for the animals who are harmed, their loved ones, those who have caused the harm, and ourselves. It's about showering love on those who suffer, and offering this prayer: *May all beings be at peace. May all beings be bathed in love and compassion.*

The whales gave this process as help to Teresa and all of us. Try it for yourself when you become overcome with emotion about the suffering or death of animals.

8

Messages from Departed Animals

*Death means wanting to be peaceful; it's knowing that your work is
done. There is no struggle because it feels right. It's tapping into a
greater whole, releasing tension, and getting off the treadmill.
It's relaxing into warmth, going to source, and being held by love itself.
It's a giant sunset, complete trust, and joining a larger force.
It's welcome and it's going home. It's all senses balancing and harmonizing
in a perfect way. It's not hearing "mind chatter" anymore.
Death means seeing the connection of all things and being the
connection of all things. It is knowing.*

—Gingerbread, Penelope's former guinea pig friend

$\mathcal{G}$etting in touch with animals who have died and are now disincarnate is similar to tuning in long-distance to animals who are still here on Earth. I usually ask the person who wants me to connect with their departed animal friend to describe the animal's former physical form as well as when, where, and how they died. Sometimes, I sense the spirit in question, and they begin communicating even without these details. However, the person's description usually helps me contact the spirit of the animal and make sure I have the right individual. Animal spirits often appear as an image of their former bodies or faces, or some recognizable aspect of their nature. They may flash thoughts, emotions, past life pictures, or whatever shows their connection with their human companion. Many people who open up to their ability to communicate with animals have similar experiences.

Sometimes, I work with deceased animals with regard to unfinished emotional matters surrounding their death. However, in most cases, I need to work with their human companion's feelings of loss or misunderstanding. Finding out what their former animal companions think and feel after death helps people move through their own grief, anger, pain, and guilt. Most animals who have made the transition are at peace. They are forgiving about the circumstances of their life and death, and feel only gratitude and love for their former family on Earth. Others are concerned that the members of their human family are okay when and after they depart.

When animals feel it's their time and they are ready to go, death is usually peaceful. They can be helped to experience a tranquil, sacred departure and state of being afterwards. Be willing to release them, thank them for jobs well-done, and recognize that the animals' missions on Earth for that life have been accomplished.

Knowing that death is not the end but a transition, a part of growth and the process of living, you won't lose contact spiritually unless you block your own awareness of the connection. You'll usually find that your departed animal friends are free and happy, and want you to share their peace and joy. Often they have been with people from life to life as friends and guides in many forms and will look after their human companions in the spiritual realm after death, or seek to reunite with them by reincarnating as another animal companion.

If animals are confused or unable to make a smooth transition, they can be helped by counseling, which then frees them to move on. I have often served as a mediator when people feel they can't fully get in touch with their animal friends themselves. However, you can learn to connect and communicate for yourself. Former animal companions are generally ready and willing to connect with the humans they love, although the spiritual connection and communication will be different from when they were on Earth in physical form. Spirits know and love each other, whether in form or formless, and can recognize each other's energies and ways of being from life to life.

When I contact animals who have died (either recently or long ago), and describe what they're doing now, I've found that even people who don't believe in life after death or reincarnation can tune in and accept the continuance. I don't think this is just the power of hopefulness or suggestion. Spirits, of whatever species, know their connection with each other, not just intellectually—they experience it from the heart. They feel and know when a genuine connection with a friend is made.

🐾 HOW ANIMALS FEEL AFTER DEATH 🐾

Once, I was the unwilling agent of death for a jackrabbit who dashed out in front of my car. Although I maneuvered the car back and forth to avoid him, I heard the thud as the tire made contact. My whole body shook with the shock, and I pulled over to the side of the road. When I contacted the former rabbit, who had left his body on impact, he laughed and commented, "It's okay. That's the third body I've lost this way. I'm used to it." His careless tone inferred that he was playing a game with cars, and he quite enjoyed it. I advised him to find some other entertainment because it was hard on people to participate in his reckless play.

I've also seen animals who were recently killed on the road, and whose spirits are not sure what happened or what to do. They hover over the body, sometimes waiting for the body to move and function again. In these circumstances, I can guide the spirit to review the incident and release any trauma or emotional fixation. I explain what happened and them on their way. You can learn how to do this, too, with practice. Communication and understanding can help animals in need after death, and it's such a relief to be able to ease their transitions.

When Chloe, Jacquelin Smith's cat companion of twenty-two years, died of old age, Jacquelin was devastated.

[Embracing Chloe,] I prayed as she was getting ready to cross over. I watched her spirit rise into the arms of the angels who gathered around her. As I held Chloe's limp body, she communicated, "I'm up here floating just below the ceiling, not in that body. I'm okay. Look at all the angels and the light. Feel the love. Hear them singing. I'm joyful to be out of my body. No more pain. Celebrate!" The room filled with light.

Even though I was grateful that Chloe was out of pain and happily winging her way into the light, I was deeply grieving. Days later, Chloe communicated, "I know you miss touching me, and I miss being touched. But both of us will be fine. We'll go on. Remember that I came into your life to help you open your heart after difficult times. I came to teach you what deeper love is. Go on in life and be open-hearted. That was my gift to you, so go on and love freely. In doing this, you honor my life."

Two months later, Etheria, my thirteen-year-old cockatiel companion, died suddenly because of an enlarged heart. I received this communication from her: "I wanted to be with Chloe in the light. I was tired and chose to leave my body. But both of us are around you. We're not dead, just transformed. Hear me sing."

What a joy when we can learn from our animal friends after death, and even hear them sing.

🐾 WILD ANIMAL CONNECTION 🐾

People may think it's horrific for a domestic animal to be killed by wild animals, but this may not be the case from the animal's point of view, as we will learn in the following examples. When Rusty and Rhea's cat, Smokey, had been missing for over a month, they asked animal communicator Kazuko Tao to check in with him.

I found Smokey's energy to be light and transparent. Smokey said he was in "heaven" and loved his peaceful state. He described to me how his death was sudden and painless as he became food for a cougar. He chose that way to move on because he wanted to experience the lightning speed of a large cat and remember what it was like to be wild. He needed to experience being independent in preparation for a lifetime as a wild animal. Smokey came into Rusty and Rhea's lives to teach them about freedom, trusting, and sticking to their own paths. He wanted them to know he cherished every moment they were together and that he was always near them, smiling with his heart wide open.

Animal communicator Sue Becker discovered that Muffin, an orange and white tabby cat who was missing from his home, had been attacked and killed by a fox. His human companion, Juanita, reported to Sue weeks later that she wanted to see the fox who had taken Muffin. She inquired of local hunters where she should look and what would be the best time of day.

On her front porch, Juanita kept a cat basket with a blanket for the comfort of her own cats and the neighborhood cats. When she went out one evening to change the water bowl, she thought there was a cat in the basket. Instead, it was a fox. As she was watching him, the fox was disturbed by some noise and trotted off.

Juanita's example shows us how our communication can travel through the universe telepathically to reach even wild animals.

DREAM CONTACT AND NOTHING TO FEAR

Animals want to comfort us and let us know they still exist. They don't want us to live with feelings of fear, despair, and isolation. They may take the opportunity to contact us in our dreams at night, when our busy minds relax and allow a receptive opening for their communication.

Martha asked Sue Becker to contact her cat, Smokey, who had passed away about six months before. Martha missed him and wanted to know how he was doing. Sue talks about her communications with Martha's cat:

Smokey said he had been with Martha quite a bit since he had left his body and that he'd done his best to support her in her grief and in life generally. He said he meets her especially at night when she sleeps and that she would remember this as dreams, although the dreams would likely be distorted memories of their visits.

Smokey reminded Martha that he was available to her at the speed of thought and that there was so much more beyond life on Earth. Physical dying, in Smokey's opinion, was really like waking up! He wanted Martha to know that he was now in his true element and although he missed his earthly life with her, he was happy to be in his spiritual home. He also wanted her to know there is nothing to fear.

As you allow yourself to realize you can connect with animals in spirit, you can begin to shed your anxiety and pain, and find comfort in the eternal being of your animals and yourself.

Barbara Molloy communicated with her poodle, Jester, after his death. She noticed he seemed more expansive than she had ever experienced him before. Several months later, while Barbara was still grieving, Jester came through again.

Listen to me. I'm not gone; I'm right here for you. You are too wrapped up in the horror of my passing, and you must get over it. I'm still here, and I'm not telling you anything you don't already know deep inside of yourself. You're just being stubborn and humanlike, but that's not the true you. It's just your outer shell and your wounded self talking.

I can help if you would just let me. I've been assisting with your emotional damage for many lifetimes. You are close to resolving this now. Relax into it. Don't fight it. Don't get caught up in the fear. Relax and breathe. Let your belly loosen. Don't resist your feelings. Breathe and let them surface. Feelings can't hurt you. The damage is already done. This is the letting go and healing phase. I'm here and I'll protect you. You're safe.

Yes, we who suffer from loss would do well to heed this advice from Jester. Relax and breathe. Let the feelings flow through. Let go and heal.

🐾 SIGNS AND VISITATIONS 🐾

Some people feel animal friends who have died and are still around. One woman experienced her two recently dead cat companions jumping on the bed at night. Other animals in spirit cause objects to move, such as photos or toys. These objects might remind the person of the departed animal and let them know the animal is there in spirit and life goes on.

Sometimes departed animals communicate through another animal in the family or even a wild animal. The eyes of the living animal might temporarily reveal the soul of the departed one, or you may feel their presence when the physical mannerisms of the living animal duplicate the gestures of the departed animal. Sounds, visions, or other synchronicities can also indicate the animal is there in spirit. Some people feel the departed animal nuzzling them. Animal communicator Kat Berard tells about how her horse confirmed his existence after death:

I've had a love affair with horses since I was very young. When I was twenty-three, an unexpected gift came my way—a thoroughbred off the track named Oh So Native (whom I affectionately named Bubba). He was retiring from racing and needed a good home. I was ecstatic to finally have my own horse companion.

Bubba was stubborn and opinionated at times, and yet he had a kind and gentle heart. He taught me how to connect with the wild, free side of myself, which I usually kept contained.

We were partners for ten wonderful years. Then, suddenly, while I was out of town, Bubba died. I was in shock and heartbroken over the loss of my beloved horse. I felt guilty for not being with him when he passed, and for not having spent much time with him in the few months beforehand because of my job.

Grief is a simple word for what I experienced. I felt like my insides were shattered glass. I could not make sense of his passing or the timing. No words could comfort me, and the knowledge that he was still with me in spirit did little to assuage my grief. However, Bubba had messages for me about the spiritual realm and our enduring connection that I could not ignore.

While he was alive, Bubba was pastured behind the house I was renting, and I was able to enjoy his beauty and presence every day. His pasture was filled for most of the year with a plant most people would call a weed, but I found it beautiful because it bore delicate purple flowers. Bubba had his own particular smell—of the woods: pine, cedar, herbs, and flowers—a unique essence that was hard to miss.

The night he died, I was talking with a spiritual mentor about Bubba in an attempt to understand why he had passed as he did. While we were talking, she suddenly became silent. I asked her what was wrong, and she said in a choked voice, "I just smelled Bubba." She lived in Colorado; I lived in Texas; and she had never met Bubba. This was the first confirmation that he was still with me and was okay.

A few months after Bubba died, I took a trip with friends first to Bali, Indonesia, and then to Australia. While in Bali, my mentor (who led the trip) ... another friend (who was with Bubba the morning he died), [and I] were in an ancient monastery carved out of lava rock at the base of a mountain. We turned a corner and there it was—that unique smell that was Bubba. Words weren't needed. We all felt the spiritual connection and the message, once again, that Bubba was well.

I traveled on to Australia, and when I visited a cattle station in the outback, I arranged a sunrise horseback ride with one of the cowhands. We rode in silence, letting the horses take us where they wanted. I was lost in thought, thinking of Bubba, because this was the first time I'd ridden since his death.

Suddenly, it came into my consciousness that we were riding through a pasture filled with purple flowers. I looked more closely and was stunned to see that they were the exact same flowers that grew in Bubba's pasture. I was halfway around the world, and this was the last thing I expected.

The message became clear: No matter where you are, they are with you. They will let you know this in some way until you get the message. Love doesn't die. The connection isn't broken just because our beloved animal (and human) companions shed their physical form.

Learning this at a deep heart level helped me move through my grief and back into living my life. It also propelled me into truly acknowledging what brought me joy, which was being with animals. This led to my animal communication work. I have since had the privilege of helping others understand what it took me so long to learn—there is no beginning or end to our connections with others.

Nancy Sondel, author and teacher, experienced phenomena that offered profound evidence of the afterlife. She writes of how three parakeets transformed her, especially following their deaths:

Though many a winged one has graced my life, three have altered it irrevocably. I bought the first, a baby parakeet, from the flock of an enterprising youngster. I didn't attempt to tame Chipper; it sufficed to see him soar. Much too soon, his vision and health declined. But in his final weeks, we found our way to each other. My eyes were his; his wings were mine. The boundaries between us dissolved.

Chipper's passing left a void, far more than I'd anticipated. I'd just tasted unconditional love and already it had vanished—like the white dove that had hovered at Chipper's grave, then followed me down a long road before ascending.

Weeks later, still grieving, I was awakened by a shimmering white light. No lamps illumined my bedroom. I wasn't dreaming or unconscious. I'd never heard of such a light except as a near-death experience.

I squinted and hid under the covers, but the white light remained. Despite my skeptical, nonspiritual orientation, I couldn't disregard this phenomenon or its recurrence during the nights that followed. Eventually, the light became a comfort.

My dreams, too, were remarkable. One displayed a red and black book, encircled by flames, which did not burn it. Given only the author's name, Balzac, I obtained the obscure, out-of-print novel. Surprisingly, the cover of *Seraphita* was exactly the colors I'd dreamed!

Blended with Swedenborg's philosophy, Balzac's novel chronicled the incarnation of a high angel or seraph (in Hebrew, meaning "to burn"). The story often paralleled my experiences—recalling, for example, an event at Chipper's funeral: "Like a dove, the soul hovered above this body."

Then a dream of strange mammals provided clues that led me to a landmark date: 60,000 years ago. During this most recent ice age, the living began burying their dead. After five million years of human evolution, Neanderthals were the first to perform this ritual. The belief in afterlife had dawned.

With these hints, I started to suspect that life continued beyond the body. It appeared that Chipper, or another Great Spirit, was providing a helpful nudge. Eventually, I read that the brilliant white light is considered a form of spirit energy. Some people meditate for years, hoping to receive such a vision. I concluded that the love I shared with one little bird was as potent as the deepest meditation.

My next feathered teacher was born in my home aviary. Now a parakeet breeder, I chose a white-with-blue nestling as my special companion. Toby's innate joy soon captivated me. Our rapport blossomed along with his speech. From a large rote vocabulary, he gradually created hundreds of phrases brimming with intelligence, imagination, humor, and love.

Toby encouraged my budding telepathic ability by nodding his head to indicate affirmation. He also blinked his eyes slowly to show me he was communicating. Sometimes I hit the mark; we even spoke the same words simultaneously!

Penelope encouraged me to regard Toby as a complete, spiritual being. Indeed, he enjoyed viewing great art with me, and my musings always enticed him. "What is spirit?" I said one day. Toby abandoned toys and food, flew to my shoulder, and peered at me as I pondered. After that, I read to him often. Whenever I mentioned angel guides or fairies dancing on the grass, Toby bobbed his head "yes."

Toby lavished me with love, infused me with laughter, and catered to my every whim. His presence strengthened and soothed me. Then, just before his sixth birthday, a mysterious illness overcame him. Several avian veterinarians were unable to change its course. As the end drew near, Toby communicated through Penelope: "When I lay my body down, I want Nancy to rise up, not suffer. I want her to reach new heights of consciousness."

Though I longed to comply, the loss was excruciating. Still, I vowed to rise up. That goal became my healing mantra. But where to begin? Simply with what I knew. Toby was embedded in my cells and my soul. He'd have wanted me to live as he had: with love and compassion, serenity and joy. So, I set my internal compass to emulate those qualities. I would embody Toby.

On this path, I could still *do* something for him as well as for myself. Toby would live not only in spirit, but also in my words and deeds. What better tribute to his life?

Yet Toby's physical absence gnawed at me. "Where is he now?" I cried daily. Dreams of Toby comforted me by night, although no white light or other clear signs appeared.

With time and meditation, I perceived Toby as part of the cosmos—invisibly present, like sugar dissolved in water. Toby and I were of the same fiber and this meant that I, too, was one with the universe. A new sense of interconnectedness enveloped me. "Each of us is all of us," I wrote.

Six weeks after Toby's funeral, I stood at home in a corner where I'd gathered mementos of his life. Heart overflowing, I felt the temperature rise in my forefinger—where Toby had usually perched. I stared in amazement as the sensation grew more intense. Toby was touching my hand!

Over the years, Toby has bestowed this gift often. However, I can never will him to manifest, not even to reassure me. Toby has taken me under his wing, a blessing to be savored as well as shared. Like sunshine and air that sustain the whole Earth, Toby doesn't belong to me alone. His love is expansive, not exclusive.

I attained this insight by degrees, starting in one of Penelope's weekend courses. Everyone sat on the grass at dusk, communing. Penelope concluded the session by saying: "Call on your animal friends whenever you wish. They'll be right there to help you."

Instantly, my hand felt hot. I gasped, surprised and grateful. A day earlier I'd wept unexpectedly because Toby had seemed so distant. Now, he radiated love and support.

Afterwards, I talked to two participants about that moment. They'd been seated on either side of me. Independent of each other, they both said my hand had appeared glowing and red hot. I'd just met these people, and they knew nothing of Toby. Yet, to our mutual delight, they experienced his living presence.

Years later, I briefly mentioned Toby to a new friend. As she and I walked in the cold winter night, Toby-Angel lit on my bare hand. With no explanation, I asked my friend if one of my hands felt hotter than the other. She stroked them both; then, staring at the spot where Toby was "perched," her eyes became enormous . . .

"Yes!" she said. "What is it?"

I explained, quietly ecstatic.

Though I need no proof that Toby still exists, I'm always thrilled when others behold his warm spirit.

Toby's legacy was in perfect harmony with Chipper's. Both demonstrated that in the natural order, life changes form but doesn't end. I contemplated this concept. Finally, logic reiterated the same truth. If matter cannot be destroyed, then soul—which is intangible—must be even more indestructible.

Something bubbled up inside of me, urging me to spread this message. I expected my next bird would help me do so. Before I recognized the newcomer, though, he nearly died in his nest. But the pint-sized parakeet survived.

The little one, white-winged and lavender-gray, fledged successfully. Yet, for weeks he didn't play or vocalize like an ordinary parakeet. He gazed at wild birds for hours. Glassy-eyed and silent, he lived with a "foot" in the other world. I sensed he had come to guide me.

I wanted to give this unusual being a name that, like him, emanated serenity. But for days the right name eluded me. Then, as I relaxed deeply, it was silently spoken: *Sachi*. How odd, I thought, until I discovered that the Japanese name means "bliss." Perfect for my Buddha-like buddy!

Sachi, however, proved extremely unyielding—the exact counterpart of Toby. Would he nibble my ear because I requested a kiss, or because Toby would have done so? Forget it!

Only four months had passed since I'd buried Toby's body. Compounding my bereavement, Sachi often preferred our aviary parakeets' company to mine. Yet, I believed Sachi cared about me, and I was committed to loving him—bittersweet as that might be.

In time, we started to merge. When I meditated or read aloud about such topics as compassion in action, Sachi perched on my shoulder. There he stayed, for up to an hour. Rare behavior in this highly active species! Eventually, I took Sachi (safe in his "castle") to the outdoor world he loved. Through him, I connected more deeply to ancient redwoods, soaring seagulls, and all creation.

Then, when Sachi was two years old, he grew sick. Medical tests revealed no cause. He recovered but sometimes fell inexplicably ill—usually after I'd finished long bursts of creative writing.

Although Sachi mirrored my intense activity, he was still the embodiment of bliss. How often he reminded me, with merely a gaze, to slow down and reflect. His small but mighty voice coaxed me back to my innermost self—that elusive, indelible, divine spark dormant within us all.

Sachi's erratic health continued for two years, until at age four he showed the irreversible signs of imminent death. I prepared to accept his passing, but I prayed he'd stay longer in his body to help me grow and nurture others. To my amazement, Sachi lived.

I grew to love Sachi without reservation, and I told him so often. Despite his taskmaster exterior, Sachi had retained an endearing juvenile habit, extremely uncommon in adult budgies: he snuggled in my turtleneck, resting or chirping, with only his tail sticking out. Now he became more cuddly, letting me rub his head, and kissing me whenever I asked. Sachi-Sage developed a unique chirp to indicate "yes"—a variation on Toby's head-nods. He even slow-blinked his eyes.

His strange ailment recurred until, at age five, Sachi was ill more often than not. Though declining, he functioned reasonably well. Then one night, he burrowed into my turtleneck, remaining for hours as I typed. The next morning, while shopping, I felt a jolt: *Sachi!*

When I returned home, I found his body lying on the cage floor, cold and stiff. My dear partner and teacher, who had carried me through the loss of Toby, had now left the Earth as well.

I partially wrapped Sachi's lifeless form and continued viewing it for days, stroking it and cherishing this symbol of our loving, transformative journey. With Sachi, I'd traveled outward on a path of service and inward towards my highest self.

On the fourth day after Sachi's passing, I wandered along the ocean. The scent of eucalyptus surrounded me, reminiscent of Toby's grave. Suddenly, it felt right to release Sachi's body, and I knew just where to do so.

The next morning, in a park overlooking the Pacific Ocean, I walked to a eucalyptus grove. In my pocket I carried scraps of paper. On these, I had written messages to bury with Sachi's body. I'd also brought a poem for his eulogy, one which portrayed the deceased as eternally present.

Tenderly, I set Sachi's body on a bed of roses, covering his remains with my notes and rich black earth. As I was replacing the eucalyptus leaves, a strong wind arose. My bag of supplies flew out of reach. I chased it as my hat, leaves, and blank journal pages scattered. After retrieving everything, I returned to the tree, then watched in awe.

The wind gained momentum, unlike anything I'd seen in the area. As I faced a tree in the eucalyptus grove, heavy gusts blew from the ocean at my far right, then past me and beyond in all directions. I stared at the grave I'd just dug, not quite covered with leaves. Suddenly, I felt a familiar tug: *Sachi.* My beloved Sachi!

I ran to a nearby field of tall, rustling grasses. Bathed in sunlight, I threw my arms open, simultaneously laughing and crying. Not tears of regret, but of rapture. Face-to-face with eternity, how could I grieve?

"I'm here with you!" I cried, while Sachi's love—all love—surged through me. I felt Sachi's laughter as he replied wordlessly: *You think you've buried me? I'm still here, bigger than ever! Bigger than that parakeet body, bigger than this canyon and ocean, bigger than all the trees you see, bigger than most everything. Wheeeee!*

In a grand crescendo, the funnel-wind roared; it seemed the ground would rip away from its core. Words thundered in my head. I recognized them from the poem I'd forgotten to read aloud: *I am a thousand winds that blow. . . .*

I gazed across the canyon, where winds bent the trees' outstretched branches. Sachi, too, was present in those distant trees. Yet, his feelings reverberated as if the words had been shouted in my ear: *You can't touch me, catch me, or hold me ... but isn't this fun? I'm dancing and flying all around you!*

I sensed that Sachi's fullness was a tremendous release, especially since I'd kept his inert body for days.

To perceive me, he continued, *remember who I am. Think you can put me in the ground? Oh no sireee, you'll never capture me. For I am spirit. I'm everywhere you see ... and everything you see not.*

In my grand life's song, Sachi's stanza echoed all that had come before: Don't be limited by the physical realm and its veil of illusion. Transcend the five senses. Trust! We're not alone in this universe; soul never dies. Our loved ones are always with us, as near as the wind's breath.

Though I needed no interpreter for what had transpired, I wanted to confirm it to encourage others. Penelope agreed to assist by phone. Disclosing nothing of the burial site or related details, I asked Penelope about Sachi's death. She relayed his response: *You think too much of a defined line of leaving the body. We're a continuum from one state to another. Even the terms "life" and "death" are human and dualistic. I've never been more alive than I am now!*

When I urged Penelope to ask about the gravesite, Sachi communicated: *I was not there. I no longer had any attachment to the body or any thought of it.*

"But," I insisted, "what happened when I laid his body in the ground?"

There's a flash of light, Nancy, as you are self-transcending, lifting out of the small ego-self and entering the Divine. And the wind answers your call, a big wind that blows from right to left as you're facing a tree. The wind comes, leaves fly, something blows up into your face. It's a great wind. . . .

Yes! Sachi *was* present at his funeral. Hearing Penelope articulate my experience in Sachi's own "words," knowing others would also rejoice in them, too, made my heart sing—as it does today.

Yet sometimes within my bounteous bliss, another reality intrudes: I'll never again cup Sachi in my palms, never feel him tickle my ear, never nestle my face against his warm feathery tummy, never hear those melodious murmurs. Whenever this stark truth erupts, I picture the cliffs where I laid Sachi's body to rest. Then the wind lifts me again and the universe cradles my soul, so that even my pain disappears.

Nothing left but gratitude and love.

Nothing, yet everything.

Not everyone experiences this kind of manifestation of an animal in spirit, but if you release your expectations and are open to the spiritual connection, anything can happen. These physical "proofs" of the eternal nature of spirit helped Nancy Sondel to further realize her own spiritual path and live in the way her birds had predicted before she was even aware of it.

Animals often cooperate in showing evidence of telepathic connection in order to spur us on our path. If a person is not ready, willing, or able to accept these signs, there is little point in manifesting in the face of the person's denial, unless a seed can be planted for future awareness. The wise spirits in animal form living among us seem to know just how to help us.

Here is another story of how a bird in spirit manifested to help deepen a person's awareness and heal her heart.

Fluffy and Mozart, Patti Henningsen's Moluccan cockatoos, had finally settled down and become loving mates after a challenging introduction period. For a few months, Patti enjoyed seeing the two birds preening and cuddling each other, but then Fluffy died from a viral disease. Patti was haunted by memories of Fluffy's deep desire to have a mate, lay eggs, and have chicks, and her desperate battle to live.

The day after Fluffy died, on a hot July afternoon, Patti sat on the front stoop looking at what had been her cockatoo's nest box and was now a flower box. She tells this story of Fluffy's manifestation:

Above the flower box in a hanging flower pot hung the dead remains of a pink impatiens. A second glance showed me that this flower, meant only to last one season, had suddenly come to life and had one tiny pink flower in full bloom. This impatiens was one-and-a-half years old and usually died during the harsh winter, but now it was blooming.

I knew it was Fluffy's soul reanimating the flesh of the flower. I brought the flower pot inside and hung it in the bedroom near Mozart's cage. A knowing, wise look from him was all I needed to be sure of this miracle.

On the anniversary of her death the following year, the same impatiens, having been dead all winter, bloomed again! I was still grieving heavily for Fluffy. Tears would well up in my eyes and my heart would seem to squeeze and tighten at the thought of the injustice of her life, waiting thirteen years to finally find happiness and then having it for only a few short months.

I lay sleepless in bed one night and rolled over to see Mozart standing on the edge of his cage. He seemed to glow in the dark as he looked down at me with a loving cockatoo smile on his face. Then he turned, walked across the cage, and sat down next to a spitting image of himself!

"Mozart," I called out. "Is that Fluffy?"

"Yeah, yeah!" he said in his little high-pitched voice, "She's here right now!"

Incredulous, I sat up. The moonlight filtered into the room through the cracks in the shade. I looked long and hard at Mozart and what must have been the ghost of Fluffy.

Mozart shifted on his feet and said, "Pat!" Then, quite firmly emphasizing each word, "Write it down."

"Yeah, yeah, I will, Motzie." I marveled at the specter of Fluffy snuggled up next to her great love, Mozart. I had never seen a ghost before, nor have I since.

Six years after Fluffy died, Mozart left, too. A few weeks later, we moved into our new house, and I wanted to put a photo of Mozart amid all the boxes to be unpacked so I could see my dear old friend.

When I picked up the little framed picture, I noticed a white blob in the photo above Mozart's head. Gazing absentmindedly at it, I realized I could see the shape of a cockatoo's beak and head, and then a dark spot where the eye would be, and wings flapping. It was Fluffy! Her spectral image had been in this photo all this time, but I had never noticed it. I ran to show the picture to my husband, Chris. "Look at this white blob right here, and do you see this dark spot?" I said.

He saw it immediately. "It's Fluffy!" he yelled. He gave me a startled hug and our eyes misted up. I looked at the calendar with another start, "And today is the day." We looked out at the sizzling hot day and waved to the pink sunset, "Namaste, Fluffy! Namaste, Mozart!"

Animals in spirit can also bridge the gap by communicating through the body of another animal. Animals may take this opportunity to "live" through another after their deaths so people can feel their palpable presence and receive their messages, even when people are able to communicate directly with the animal in spirit. The deceased animals have a need to reach the people they love deeply, too. Animal communicator Pamela Au tells how her cat used another cat as a medium to connect with her after his death:

Samson was a white feral cat with a black spot on his head and a black tail. He was extremely thin and had blotches of fur missing. He appeared one day on my patio refrigerator asking for help, and I began to feed and care for him. After several months, he trusted me fully and allowed me to pet him as well as pick him up. He began to regain his health.

After he had asked permission, he showed up with his "wife," Samantha, and two children. They were all feral. He [brought] them everyday to eat.... Eventually, he began to live on top of the refrigerator. We nicknamed him "the refrigerator cat." One day, Samantha asked me if she could have her babies on the patio. A place was made for her, and she gave birth to two kittens. One kitten died and the other stayed with me.

For a cat whose mother had abandoned him at a young age, Samson was an expressive, talkative cat and an amazing father and surrogate mother. He taught his kitten how to hunt and play, and even allowed him to nurse. Of course, Samson didn't have any milk, but it was comforting to the kitten. Samson could figure out how to open things, and he could climb through the windows when they were open as little as four inches.

Sadly, Samson was a wanderer and would go places where he should not have been. He came home one day with a swollen abdomen. He had been poisoned. He begged for help, but it was already too late. When Samson passed on, he told me he would return.

Within two weeks of his passing, an orange feral cat appeared on the patio. I had never seen him before. He sat on top of the refrigerator the same way Samson used to do. When it was dinnertime, he waltzed right into the house and headed for the kitchen as if he had been there before. The way he walked and talked gave me chills. When I looked at him, I didn't see a feral cat. I saw Samson, whose spirit was present in this cat. He had come back to say goodbye and thank me for providing a home for his family and nurturing him. Samson was full of gratitude because he had never experienced love before. He was still doing his job as a good dad and making sure everyone was alright. All of the cats behaved as if he actually was Samson.

The orange cat knew my house. He knew me and my family, as well as Samson's family. He allowed me to pet him and spoke in the same way Samson had. He remained in and around our house for three weeks and then was gone.

One month later, he appeared briefly. This time, he was no longer Samson. He was a complete stranger. He would not let us pet him and seemed disoriented. It was as though he didn't understand what had happened to him. He refused to come in the house and would only eat outside when no one was around.

Samson had used the orange cat as the medium to come back to us for a short period of time.

There are many instances of animals who are no longer in the physical body communicating through other animals in the family, or even through wild animals. Some animals, as described in Pamela's experience, are brief "incarnations." Sometimes, a living animal will take on the energy patterns and role of a departed animal in order to fill the vacuum left behind. This is often accompanied by confusion or disorientation for the living animal. The animal may also be grief-stricken, and this is his way of coping with the loss. You can usually handle this kind of confusion by letting the living animal know you appreciate him for himself and that he doesn't have to imitate the departed animal in order to be loved. Showing compassion for the living animal's grief and treating him tenderly can go a long way towards healing the wound and restoring balance.

🐾 PROFOUND TRUTHS 🐾

Animals in spirit often communicate that they are relieved to have been released from their painful bodies. They also give us profound truths about the nature of life and death.

Annette was on tranquilizers when she called animal communicator Jacquelin Smith. Her cat, Karl, had died a week before from a stroke while having his teeth cleaned. About six months before, four of the other animals who lived with her had died suddenly because someone poisoned them. Karl communicated these messages for Annette.

My stay with you was the best part of my life. I was learning to trust humans again. Some experiences were good and some were not so good, but I could always count on you. We have experienced a number of close lifetimes together. I missed you, and we both welcomed being together again to learn about ourselves and each other.

My body was aching and I hurt in my bones. I decided to leave my body so I wouldn't have to suffer in a different way later on. My death was a big shock because it was so sudden. I didn't know I had left my body for several days. But when I walked up to you and you didn't respond, I knew. It isn't easy for me to be out of the body and separated from you in this way. I whisper thoughts into your ears at night and at dawn. I will be around for awhile, but then I will move on to different experiences.

You certainly haven't had an easy road to walk. It's time for you to love and nurture yourself. In some ways, I gave you what you couldn't give yourself. But now you're ready to follow your heart's desire.

Remember my bright eyes, for this will help us connect. If you think a thought to me I will hear. Listen for my thoughts. I may come to you through images and feelings, so relax and trust them.

I send bushels of love. I feel scared and confused at times, so please send me love and light that's like the sun I always loved so much. I am glad to be free of my body and yet I still feel sad.

Just as trees bear fruit, we will spring forth again bearing fruit. We will be together again. I leave you with the image of a multifaceted diamond, which reflects the light in all its aspects.

When Jacquelin spoke this last sentence about the diamond, Annette sobbed for a long time and then said:

All this is incredible. I have been through hard times in my life and am just learning to love and think about my heart's desires. Karl did love the sun more than my other animals. We often gazed into each other's eyes. He had unusually bright eyes. His amazing message about the diamond pierced my heart. No one in the world knew about the diamond. Before I buried Karl, I laid him in a wooden box and put one of my diamond earrings between his paws.

These messages from Karl to Annette helped her see the light of hope in the midst of darkness and grief. Annette was sad because she missed Karl, but she was also ecstatic because now she knew he was alive in spirit.

To tap into the loving lessons and messages from animals who have gone on, practice the techniques of animal communication. Spend quiet time breathing deeply, feeling your connection to the Earth through your feet on the ground, and opening your heart and mind to your animal friend in spirit.

Have a pen and paper ready to write down whatever comes through as you feel the connection with your animal friend. Let your hand move in automatic writing fashion without censoring or trying to make sense of the words. Just let the writing come through. If you are right-handed, you can also try writing with your left hand, which helps tap into the intuitive side of the brain. At first, the writing may be hard to decipher. That's okay. Continue writing, and you may be surprised by what you receive. Your animal friend will probably take this receptive opportunity to communicate to you all that he or she wishes you to know.

Animals usually communicate comforting, loving messages after they pass on. They give good advice about life from their expanded perspective.

Camille was having trouble forgiving herself for having two of her dogs, Wally and Pablo, put to sleep and only six months apart. She contacted Karen Taylor to speak with them to find out how they felt about it and where they were now. Karen relayed this message from Wally:

We are together as one energy is with another energy, and therefore we are oneness. The actions of the past do not affect us here. No forgiveness is required because there is nothing to be forgiven. You did exactly what needed to be done at that moment in time. It was perfection.

Do not hold onto those moments any longer. They do not serve you. Move away from that kind of thinking. It's done. Be here now and forever in the present. Enjoy today and tomorrow. Enjoy it again, for it will be another today. The past and future are of no matter because it's always now.

Karen also received a message from Pablo:

Yes, we are of the *now*. We are in everything in this Universe and the next—the "Great Isness," which is being created in every moment. There is nothing and there is everything. The end of my body-life moved me into this experience, which is where we all are in between our physical experiences for as long as we choose. Your helping me get here is of no consequence because I would have found my way here eventually, as all beings do. It brought me great peace to be released from a body that no longer functioned properly. I am grateful for your assistance.

🐾 TAKING CARE OF US 🐾

It's amazing and heartwarming to find out how profoundly animals feel about their mission to care for us, even after death. Animal communicator Karla McCoy consulted with a woman about a Boston terrier named Rosie, who had died about a month before.

Rosie was worried about her human companion's health. I got from Rosie that the woman needed to get to a doctor as soon as possible. It felt like her heart area was affected. It was not serious yet, but it could become serious. I experienced great relief when the spirit of the woman's dog confirmed my feeling.

I tried to relay this to the woman gently. I said her dog wanted to know how she was feeling. She told me she had some nausea but other than that she felt fine. I looked directly at her and told her she needed to get checked out. Maybe it was nothing, but if there was a problem and it was caught in time, it would not become serious. She assured me she would.

Two weeks later, I received a phone message from the woman. She informed me that a small cancerous lump had been found in her breast, but it had been caught in time. She thanked me through her tears and said she would never have gone to the doctor if it had not been for me talking to her dogs. She said I had played a part in saving her life.

Casta, animal communicator Georgina Cyr's former boxer dog companion, communicated this universal lesson about the purpose of animals in our lives:

The spirits of animals and all beings are made up of love. It's not just "love," but pieces of love all put together into a particular form that shapes a particular being. When a being starts its form, it's made from the One Great Love. As the form takes shape, it opens up to giving and receiving love. The being holds the spirit, and the spirit's whole purpose is to gather the love and allow it to grow and become one with the One Love. It grows bigger and bigger until there is only love.

Animals who live with humans have taken their forms specifically to help us with individual human love. They help us learn about it and share, give, and receive it. They have the capability to help us generate greater love than any other form because they are able to share unconditional love with us. Animals usually have shorter lives than humans, and several animals might work in different ways to help generate this depth of love within a human's lifetime.

We know and value the purpose of being in a physical body, which is to help raise the vibration of the physical dimension. Love will lift the vibration.

When animal companions leave their bodies permanently, they are trying to help humans learn that the spirit just goes into a different dimension and exists in a different form. Many animal spirits choose to come back into a physical body again and go on to another human to raise that human's vibration. The understanding, compassion, unconditional love, and acceptance of animals can help humans move past their boundaries and self-imposed restrictions.

As animals touch every human spirit, the unconditional love available grows larger and stronger, affecting the vibration and level of love in the universe. This helps to spread love even to beings who are not aware of it. Animals want to become so full of the love they share with us that together we can help all spirits heal themselves and become whole again.

Dixie Golins, who studied animal communication with me, received a message from her royal python snake, Wise One, the evening before her sister's cat, Charlotte, was euthanized. Dixie had been keeping in touch with Charlotte throughout her illness and especially during the last days of her life on Earth. She was feeling a lot of sorrow the evening before Charlotte's passing. While she was feeling this grief, her snake came out of his hide box and looked at her intently. Dixie could tell that Wise One had something important to say, so she sat down and listened to his message about death.

Death is no more than an exhale. There is a rhythm and a cycle to all life. Spirit becomes form becomes spirit. And so it goes. To grieve for the passing of the form is to miss the magnificence of the spirit, which is as fluid and ever-present as liquid light. There is eternity in all of us. We have no beginning and no end, and we are eternally present in all moments of time simultaneously. We are so much bigger and more beautiful than any of us could ever imagine. When someone who is dear to us dies, there is a particle of light that leaves our heart and a particle of light that also returns. We are part of each other. This exchange is our gift of love to each other. I feel softness in your heart for the one who is to change. To die is to step into the eternal *now*.

Death is a gateway into the mysteries of life. Each of us stands on the threshold of death each day. We die a little each day and are in a constant state of change. There is no part of us that remains static. We are in a constant state of motion, constantly changing, constantly becoming anew. We are the ebb and flow of the tides, the waxing and waning of the moon. We are in a constant state of becoming. We hold eternity in every cell. The vastness of all that is exists within us.

There are many aspects to death. Humans focus only on the death of the body. There is much more to death than this. Death is a passage from one realm of being to another. The transition is fluid, gentle, and easy. The shifting of form comes naturally to all life. Only humans resist it because they fear the unknown. Death comes to all of us. It's the gentle one who awaits us at the end of our journey. We release ourselves into its loving presence and awaken to the magnificence of our expansive selves. Death is the gift of life.

9

Animals Returning

Whatever may fall stays not long on the ground.
All death holds new life, the circle complete.

—Turkey vulture

$\mathcal{M}$any people recognize their current animal friends as former animal or even human companions. When people ask me to check this for them, almost always I can confirm their recognition or suspicion by connecting with the being in question. Sometimes, people recognize their animal friends through similar mannerisms or actions. Most of all, they recognize the energy of the particular being, even if the breed or species is different. They may also experience a distinct feeling of having been with an animal before.

In counseling sessions, animals often communicate about other lifetimes they have lived when asked about a subject that relates to a former life. They are not usually aware of or thinking about past lives because they are here to enjoy life in their present form. However, most animals are open to remembering when it can help resolve a problem or forge a deeper connection with the people in their current lives. The veils of human socialization cause most people to forget and then deny their own previous lives, even when an experience jogs a memory to the forefront. In past life regression counseling, however, many people pierce the veils of eternal existence and remember.

I have experienced my own past life memories in regression sessions and in flashback visions stimulated by places and circumstances similar to those in the past life. In counseling sessions, I have dissolved present life emotional issues and even physical difficulties by viewing and releasing past life traumas and realizing their relationship to current situations. As a counselor, I have also assisted countless people and animals in viewing aspects of their past lives, which can precipitate profound emotional and physical releases that instantly and dramatically change or improve chronic problems and even illnesses. The journey through different lifetimes can give us opportunities as spirits to experience many aspects of reality in many cultures and even different types of bodies.

While recalling a past lifetime in China, Jacquelin Smith wrote down a series of letters, or symbols, in a column. She asked a friend to show them to an ancient language professor at a university. He was taken aback and said every symbol was from a particular ancient dialect in China. After this experience, she knew past lives were real. She has never studied Chinese.

I have often been privileged to help in the transition after death, relieving trauma or confusion for the animal spirits or humans. Animal communicators can also help people and their animal friends reunite, if that's what the people and animals want. We all have the capacity to tune in and recognize beings we have known before.

Why would an animal come back to the same person?

Sometimes it's to continue their mission to help, guide, and serve. Some animal friends feel you can't do without them! One cat told me seventeen years was not enough time to take care of her human companion and make sure she became enlightened. She would need at least another seventeen years, so she appeared again in cat form to continue her task.

Often, animals do not come back immediately but have other things to do in the spiritual realm. Some may need to reincarnate elsewhere, sometimes even as humans. You may see them again many years later, after they have lived other lives. Your association may even go back hundreds or thousands of years.

Our animal friends are often our spiritual guides in life, helping us through hard times and teaching us about love and joy. They are often quite aware of their purpose and may continue to take care of us from the spiritual realm, or they may reincarnate in a new physical form—if that is the best way for the beings involved to learn from each other.

A woman called me a week after her cat friend, Celeste, had disappeared out of the yard. I perceived and described the cat's location next to a garage in some dirt and brush. I sensed she had been attacked by a raccoon. The woman said the description fit her next door neighbor's yard. She went there and found her cat dead and mangled. The woman was relieved to know what had happened to Celeste but was obviously distraught about her loss.

I tuned into Celeste as a spirit and discovered that when she was attacked she left her body instantly. Celeste did not experience the pain of the struggle, but she hung around her body for a while, hoping her cat form would get up again so she could go home.

The woman felt guilty and grieved the circumstances of her cat's death. I let her know that Celeste did not hold anything against her. I said Celeste was doing well now and wanted to reincarnate and be her cat companion again.

It's common for animals to want to be with the same people over and over. They may have been with each other through different lifetimes in various roles, nonhuman and human. Even if the bodily forms and other characteristics are different, spirits recognize each other by their energies, their communication, and their way of being.

Barbara Janelle's cat, Wimsey, was smart, curious, and people-oriented. Two years after she died, another cat, Magic Bailey, came into Barbara's life. Barbara noted that both cats were black, although Wimsey's body was smaller, finer, and more fluid in movement, and she was female. Magic was male, quite large, and somewhat awkward in his body. Barbara held Magic and knew he was Wimsey reincarnated. She recognized the ancient wisdom, focus, and determination of her powerful teacher, even though the personalities of the two cats were quite different.

Friends like to be together and spirits of like mind and purpose travel similar paths, often finding each other from life to life. We may not be with the same beings every lifetime, but most of the people and animals we are close to have been with us before in one or many previous lives.

Other animals have traveled with us as animal companions previously or have been human friends or relatives in previous lives. This sometimes makes roles confusing; for example, when you have a dog who acts like your mother or a cat who sees herself as your lover. Recognizing and acknowledging the past connection is usually all it takes to establish a healthy, balanced relationship in the current incarnation. Spirit is infinite and can be anything, but bodies, especially of different species, relate to each other within certain understandable boundaries, according to the culture of their species.

Many members of my animal family have returned over the years to help me teach humans about interspecies communication. When my sweet hamster friend, Thomas Thimble, left his body, he ascended to angelic realms and sent warm, white, golden energy back to us. It appeared he would not reincarnate again. A few months later, I was moved to get a new rat companion after my others had died. A beautiful soul named Kiri came along. As I was describing her sweetness to a friend, I realized she was Thomas Thimble returned. What an unexpected joy to have him back as a female rat!

🐾 CHANGING ROLES 🐾

Unresolved past life challenges can cause problems to surface that need to be faced in this life. Carol called me about her two-year-old dog, Natasha, who seemed emotionally troubled and suffered from one physical problem after another. Natasha was a therapy dog and helped emotionally disturbed people. Carol thought this might be too stressful for her.

Contacting and communicating with Natasha was an adventure. She was an amazing being of great awareness and spiritual depth. She was close to Carol and felt a deep bond with her. Her problems this lifetime were triggered by her relationship with Carol and the therapy work. We did some healing for her present problems, and it surfaced that these issues were based in a previous life.

Natasha recalled a lifetime in ancient Egypt when she had been involved in temple healing. Her present human companion, Carol, had been a priestess healer in the temple. Natasha was Carol's male assistant and was in charge of the temple dogs, who assisted in healing the people who came to the temple. These dogs were extremely sensitive and spiritually aware. When people came to the temple with physical, emotional, or spiritual problems, the dogs would take on the ailments to relieve the people. Sometimes this resulted in severe suffering or even death for the dogs. Natasha loved the dogs and felt guilty about the pain they suffered.

Natasha released much grief and other painful emotions as she recounted the feelings, events, and patterns of that lifetime. She realized she felt responsible, and as a dog this lifetime, she felt she had to suffer in the same way to assist humans.

As the pain of the incident lifted, Natasha declared she did not need to sacrifice herself anymore. She advised Carol that both of them needed a break from feeling so responsible for others and trying to heal them, while neglecting themselves. Natasha told Carol through me, "I need to relax and just experience joy, with no demands or commands. Perhaps our time with each other is ending, or maybe we can laugh and be carefree together. I feel relieved. Peace will come from being together."

Carol experienced incredible energy during our long-distance communication and healing with Natasha. She said the dog had been outside when we started but had come into the room and commanded that Carol sit and meditate with her. They sat together throughout the experience, while Natasha visibly went through changes.

Our roles can also change from life to life, depending on the chosen design for our journey. Jacquelin Smith gives some interesting examples of changing roles:

A delightful Panamanian parrot, Shirley, had shared several lifetimes with her present human companion, Larry. In one life, she was a scarlet macaw in South America, and Larry was a young Indian boy who helped heal her broken wing. Over the years, they grew close and telepathically communicated with one another. When the boy became a man, he had a wife who gave him three children. The macaw felt displaced because of difficult changes and circumstances in that life. Later on, the macaw was brokenhearted because she outlived her human friend.

In another life, Shirley was Larry's human daughter. She lived in Africa with her father, who studied plant life. Larry's wife died from a fever when the daughter was three. Later the daughter went to England, became a nurse, and married. She and her husband returned to her father's home after many years. When her father died, she and her husband buried him in Africa.

In her present existence, Shirley conveyed how important it is to be with Larry because of their strong soul ties. I could feel the intimate link between them. They chose to be together again in this life to continue their experience.

Shirley and Larry live in the city this time around, which is quite a change of scenery. Their connection must be especially close for Shirley to choose life as a parrot living in a large city. She may outlive Larry again because parrots can live sixty or more years in captivity.

One time Shirley got out of the apartment and was flying around Chicago. Larry ran a lost and found ad offering a reward for her return. When Shirley was safely returned, Larry's response was, "I knew she and I were destined to be together. It must be divine intervention when an animal, especially a bird, gets lost in a giant city with millions of people and is found and returned."

While at a zoo one day, I felt an unusually strong heart-to-heart connection with a gorilla, who had been caught in the wild. I asked her if she would like to chat. She silently voiced how much she enjoyed being outside in the air and sitting on the green grass, especially after being contained inside a building in a cage at another zoo.

She shared some past life experiences with me: "I have been a gorilla many times, but not always. I was a man who studied and lived with gorillas. I wanted to totally understand what they feel and how they perceive their world, so I chose to be a gorilla. I am learning a tremendous amount and will come back again as a human to verbally teach humans about gorillas. Because I am in captivity, I am learning about gorillas and also teaching humans about gorillas.

Charlie is a poodle who communicated that one reason he and his human companion, Ted, were together again was to learn from each other about similar personality patterns. Charlie had been a stray about two years old when he found Ted. "We vibrate to the same tone, light, and rhythm," said Charlie. "To try and put this into words limits it. Feel it and you'll understand."

Charlie went on to say to Ted: "Let's share our time together in understanding. You as human and me as dog in this life can know the new kind of closeness we agreed to share before being born in these bodies. It's an advantage at times to be in an animal body, other than human, to understand relationships. I hope we connect in deeper ways than we have in some other lives. Our past lives number many. It's important to know we teach and learn from each other as equals."

Contrary to certain human philosophies, these examples show that being an animal is not lowlier than being human. Spirits, whether in human or animal form, can have high ideals and consciously serve to advance others.

🐾 IMITATION LIFETIME 🐾

Animals can imitate the other species that surround them as they are growing up, but unusual behavior patterns can also be due to past life influence. One of my rabbit companions died and decided to return to my household as a guinea pig. For the first few days at home, she hopped like a rabbit until she got familiar with the patterns of her new body. I met a cat whose recent past life as a rabbit showed in her mannerisms. She had adapted what she liked about being a rabbit to her current cat form. A skittish dog had a hard time adjusting to life with humans because he thought and acted like the deer he had been in his last life.

We can't assume that behaving like another animal is always because of a past life experience as that animal. Telepathic communication with particular animals will reveal their unique experiences and reasons for being the way they are.

When people truly listen to animals rather than human projections or preconceived notions, animals visibly and favorably respond, and change for the better. When you practice receiving communication from living animals, you can tell if your impressions are accurate because the animal responds positively and the behavior situation becomes easy to resolve with the understanding of what is really going on. Communication with deceased animals is less tangible, although often animals will give details that correspond to their former physical reality. Communication from deceased animals also resonates as true in the hearts of their human companions, and the truth received helps resolve the emotional and spiritual aspects of death and dying.

Many animal companions, who act like humans and are interested in and responsive to people, have lived as humans previously or have been domesticated animals who assisted people. Because of positive past life experiences in human society, they easily adapt to life with humans. They're tuned in to the way people think and may even speak mentally in human language. This parallels how some young, extraordinarily talented humans have revived or simply carried on the abilities they mastered in a previous life. Although many animals are not aware of the influences of past lives, they usually open up quickly to their past life memories when asked about them, unlike more socially conditioned humans. Knowing about past life influences can help you understand and resolve current problems.

One woman called me because her sheltie, Nick, refused to pick up the dumbbell, an object used for retrieval in dog training. When I walked in the door, Nick treated me as he did other humans, with the condescending attitude, "Oh, another one of them."

I sat down, talked to the woman, and then looked at Nick. When he finally deigned to take notice of me and realized that I could understand what he was thinking, his reaction was comical. Nick slowly backed up toward the corner and stared at me, dumbfounded. His human companion was amazed at his reaction and said that she'd never seen him act like that before. Nick didn't want people to know what he was thinking, and he never expected to meet a human who could understand his thoughts.

When he got over his shock, Nick said he thought human and dog games were beneath him. When I questioned him further, he recalled his last life as a champion race horse, when he felt far superior to everyone. His human companion told me that the carriage of his neck was different from other shelties. Nick, the dog, even stamped his feet like a horse.

I respected his dignity as a spiritual being, acknowledged his self-image, and then reoriented him to his current situation. Nick didn't realize how much he'd been acting out his last life. As he became more aware of what he was doing and more relaxed, his arrogance lessened.

It turned out that Nick actually enjoyed the dog training, but he had to show his human companion he was in charge instead of just cooperating with her and having a good time. She gave Nick a lot of loving care and attention, so I talked to him about returning the same to her. It helps if people make training a fun game for the dog instead of an all-too-serious effort, but Nick's human companion was already doing this. It was the dog's attitude that got in the way. Now that Nick had released his defensiveness toward her and life, he was more willing to cooperate in dog training competition.

Opus was found as a stray kitten in Las Vegas, Nevada. He was wild, but his human companion had a special love for him and called me for assistance. When I consulted with the cat long-distance, Opus was six years old, neutered, and weighed twenty pounds.

Looking with him at his past, I saw that his Maine coon mother had been dumped in the desert and survived as a feral cat. She mated with a domesticated tomcat but abandoned her two kittens after about four weeks. Only one survived—Opus. The person who found him lived in an apartment building that did not allow cats, and Opus was yowling almost nonstop. She called me because she couldn't make him stop this behavior, which could mean eviction for both of them.

I saw that Opus needed contact with the Earth and outdoors, but this was impossible for the woman to accommodate. Opus became wild if she took him anywhere, even on a harness, plus she feared being discovered by the landlord.

This woman and her cat had been American Indians together in past lives, living on the Earth in harmony with nature. They had made a pact to meet again. Opus later became a mountain lion and then a wild animal trainer of tigers and lions. As a trainer, he loved the cats but had a hard time getting along with people. He later lived as a bob-cat and then was born to his current Maine coon mother. He had a conflict between being close to nature (and avoiding human civilization) and his desire to be with his current human companion.

I felt that Opus needed some kind of outdoor enclosure, where he could touch the Earth and dissipate his wild energy. His human companion couldn't provide this in her current situation, and she couldn't afford to move. I suggested she thoroughly acknowledge and understand his feelings, supply a large box of earth and grass for him to use, and promise to provide a future outdoor safe space for him when possible. She reported to me weeks later that after our consultation, Opus yowled only once and was quiet when she acknowledged him.

A rather unmanageable cat named Emily fled from people. I noticed she was wearing a flea collar. This was a source of irritation, not only because of the toxic effects but because it reminded Emily of a gruesome death that contributed to her current unruliness. First, I removed the flea collar and then counseled Emily. She had been a feral cat living in the woods during her last life, and she had gotten caught in a wire snare, where she hung and struggled for hours before dying. I worked with her to discharge the fear and pain from these memories. Her human companion told me later that Emily drastically changed after our consultation. Instead of running away or scratching and biting, Emily now curled up in her lap and enjoyed affection.

These examples illustrate how we sometimes continue old patterns, and how we can have incredible spiritual relationships with each other from life to life, no matter what species form we take. While there is no guarantee that an animal companion will come back to you, it's another possible connection to consider. You can ask them to return, if it's right for them and they have a mission to be with you. One way or another, we will meet again and are connected always in spirit.

🐾 PROOF 🐾

Animals sometimes provide evidence of their return that is hard to deny. They may also return through surprising, fortuitous, or seemingly magical avenues. Here are a few examples, first from Betty Lewis, animal communicator and Great Dane and whippet breeder, who tells a fascinating story of her dog's return.

Tassel was a special brindle Great Dane. Despite a broken leg at the age of three months, she had recovered and was adequately sound. By the age of three she had attained her Tracking Dog (TD) title. Tassel even had a special "trick." We had cowbells hanging on the dogs' collars so we could hear them in the wooded fenced yard when they were outside. We put the collars on the dogs when they went out, but inside, the collars hung on a hook by the door. Tassel was the only dog in our thirty years of breeding Great Danes who had learned to ring the bells to ask to go outside.

Suddenly, disaster struck. Tassel came down with a fever of unknown origin. Nothing from the arsenals of holistic or allopathic medicine was able to bring the fever under control, and we lost her.

We had previously decided to get a whippet, but put it off for various reasons. We started the process of looking for a puppy, only to have an older dog offered to us. Her name was Heaven. I was in such a state that anything more subtle might have been ignored, but even I couldn't miss the significance of her name.

Heaven was nine months old when she came to live with us. Within two hours of being in our home, she deliberately went to the collars and rang the bells!

Shortly after Heaven arrived, Tassel came to me in a dream. She said she was sending me her halo. There was no doubt in my mind that Heaven was to be renamed Halo and that she was a present from Tassel.

Halo gave me a lovely litter of puppies, and we enjoyed participating in many competitive events together. I expected her to live until about fifteen because whippets are known to be a healthy breed.

When Halo was about eight, I started thinking about another whippet puppy because I missed competing in the show ring. I didn't pursue it seriously, though, because we were comfortable as a family. We had two Great Danes and two whippets. I didn't do more than occasionally think about it. However, Halo, evidently considered my thoughts as a fait accompli, but I didn't learn this for several weeks.

One day, during our weekly grooming, I noticed a lump in Halo's groin. Within four days, there were lumps all over her. From my training as a veterinary technician, I was pretty certain I was looking at lymphoma. A veterinary exam confirmed my suspicions, and I looked for a way to help her overcome the disease. We tried a myriad of holistic approaches and some allopathic suggestions, but nothing changed her condition.

Halo had an agenda I couldn't alter. From the first lump to the end, it was only five short weeks and then she was gone.

We all cried; it was so unfair. I'd spent thirty-five years with Great Danes, a breed with an average lifespan of eight years, only to lose the dog I'd expected to live forever at eight and a half.

Halo wasn't gone, however. She had a specific plan and was intent on fulfilling her designated role. She told me about it after leaving her physical body.

First of all, she was indignant that she wasn't the only whippet in the family. She came into our family agreeing to the already existing Great Danes, but she came from a pack of seventeen whippets and she didn't want it repeated. She had consented to having a litter of puppies, but she was *not* aware we were going to keep one of them. She didn't think this was part of the original bargain she'd made, but since Shimmer was *hers*, she let it go. However, when I started thinking about *another* puppy, she decided it was time to take a stand.

This wasn't the larger agenda, however. She told me she really thought she could be more useful to me and the other dogs if she was a guide from the spirit realm.

The first task she set herself to was finding me a whippet puppy. The breeder Halo had come from had a litter I was interested in, but there were only three bitches and I had third pick. From the first time I saw pictures of the puppies, I knew there was only one of the three I would consider, so I'd pretty much resigned myself to not being able to get a puppy from this litter. I have some pretty specific requirements, so I knew if I didn't get this one, it would be quite some time before circumstances would present themselves for me to get any puppy.

So I said to Halo, "If you really died so I could get a puppy, please make it possible for this puppy to be mine." The next morning I received an e-mail saying, "If you want the puppy, come pick her up today."

Within a few days of the new puppy, Kiah's, arrival, she deliberately went to the bells and rang them! And so the cycle of life continues.

Mary Stoffel found proof of reincarnation in the demonstrated knowledge of her new kitten. Her example also shows that we can help ourselves connect with our animal friends in spirit by learning shamanic journeying:

Samson, our ten-year-old orange cat, was killed by a car on the road in front of our house on a weekend when I was gone. It was difficult because

I could feel him everywhere and kept expecting him to walk into the house. I did a shamanic journey to his spirit and saw him in his perfect physical form. He was waiting for me. I asked him about his death, and he said it was truly an accident. He just didn't see the car coming. He also said we had more work to do together and he was planning to reincarnate. I told him that as wonderful as it was to feel close to him, he really needed to go completely to the other side so he could come back as soon as possible. He looked at me intently and said, "That's right! I forgot!" and ran straight into the light. After that journey, I didn't feel his spirit around at all, but I knew he would find me again.

I figured out the time necessary for him to be born and be old enough to leave his mother, and I started paying attention to signs and intuitive feelings around that time. One night, I was hosting a monthly animal communication practice session and a student brought up a case study about a Siamese kitten she had found two days earlier. She was a park ranger and someone had thrown the kitten out of a car. He was a vocal kitten, and she wanted to know if she was supposed to find him a home or whether he was supposed to stay with her. As soon as she started talking, I could hardly contain myself. I knew immediately it was Samson, and this was confirmed when we checked in with him. My friend promised to bring the kitten over the next day. Samson was so relieved that he stayed in contact with us for the rest of the practice session. Samson arrived the next day as a cute little Siamese kitten with a big voice.

We have a cat door that goes from the downstairs family room into the laundry room, but it's not obvious where this door is. The cats have to go around a corner of the room and under a bookcase to find the door. The day after he arrived, Samson followed me all over the house while I did chores, including the laundry. I really didn't want him in the laundry room at that time because he was so little and I was afraid he'd get lost, hurt, or buried under a pile of clothes. I didn't let him follow me and shut the "people" door in his face. It took him about three seconds to go around the corner and in through the cat door. He remembered where it was!

Anita Curtis's clients, Mr. and Mrs. Williams, were devastated by the loss of their precious dog, Katie. Anita tells about how Katie proved she had returned:

Katie had the unusual habit of hiding one of her biscuits in the sofa cushions. If Mrs. Williams dug the biscuit out and offered it to her, Katie would turn her head to the side as if she didn't see it. If Mrs. Williams was cleaning and threw the biscuit out, Katie would replace it at once.

Katie had promised to come back to them in a new healthy body. She said she would come back as a rescued dog at the pound. Mr. and Mrs. Williams called me every week to see if it was time. Finally, Katie told me it was time to go look for her. The Williams called the next day to tell me one of the dogs at the pound was Katie, and they had brought her home without any question. As soon as they got home, they offered the new dog a biscuit. She took it, dashed into the living room, and buried it in the cushions of the sofa. Mrs. Williams pulled the biscuit out and offered it to the dog and then she cried as the dog turned her head to the side. Katie was back home.

Sometimes animals return to the same family after some time, despite other obstacles. Animal communicator Cindy Wenger tells how she assisted in the reunion of a whippet named Febe with her client Thelma Boyd:

Febe had made a special connection with Thelma Boyd. She accompanied Thelma as she did chores each day: cleaning the house, shopping, and caring for two young daughters. Every evening, Febe would nestle in the crook of Thelma's arm and fall asleep.

Thelma's husband, Mike, was a career naval officer, and over the years the family moved to various homes. The one constant for Thelma was Febe. Each new home the family moved to was accented by flower gardens planted by Thelma, with Febe's constant supervision and approval. After years of devotion, Febe died in Thelma's arms and was buried in one of their beloved gardens.

During consultations over the years, Febe would pop in to validate that she was indeed stopping by to visit and was aware of what was going on with each family member. She wanted to comfort Thelma, who was sad about Febe's physical absence. With the passing of over a decade and numerous moves, Thelma was concerned that Febe would lose track of the family. However, during our consultations Febe always assured Thelma that she knew exactly where the family was.

Mike, now retired, suggested they should not add another animal to the already large household menagerie of cats, birds, fish, a gecko, and dogs. He wanted to begin downsizing because of Thelma's severe asthma.

So, it was quite a surprise when Mike came home with a female whippet. Mike felt the dog would not be troublesome and would meld into the family. The other animals immediately accepted their new "sister." Although apprehensive, Thelma, too, accepted Sable and they bonded instantly.

Sable had been with her new family for a couple of days, when Thelma called me for a consultation. When I connected with Sable, I immediately received the message "I am Febe. I have returned." She showed me a picture of her sleeping contentedly with Thelma. I relayed Sable's message and told Thelma that she had her girl back.

Thelma validated that Sable has virtually all the characteristics of Febe, including her propensity to sleep in the crook of Thelma's arm, her love of shopping, and assisting with the care of the flower beds. Sable also continually checks on Thelma when she has breathing or coughing spells.

Some animals demonstrate their return through mystical, symbolic events that reach deep into the hearts of their human companions. Gayle Nastasi remembers 1996 as a pivotal year that propelled her onto a new path as an animal communicator. Of all the events of that year, none was as traumatic, shocking, or influential as the death of her young dog.

Jai was a saluki, a four-year-old black and silver momma's boy. He was in apparent perfect health, and he ran, played, laughed, and danced. Jai was a lively, sparkling joy.

On the morning of September 7, at around 10:00 AM, Jai's light went out with a flare of tragedy that rocked our world. He had been out to play and came in happy. He lay down in the living room, where his sister, Dancer, and my two children were relaxing. I turned to answer some e-mails, heard a thud and cry, and spun around to see Jai on his side having a seizure. My children stood and stared. "What's wrong with him, Mommy?" eleven-year-old Jess asked. I told her not to worry. He was having a seizure and would be all right.

But I was wrong. Jai's breathing stopped. He was dead.

Jess made the call for help. I could only focus on doing CPR to bring him back. I pumped his heart and breathed for him for forty minutes, while Jess called her father and my mother, and got her little brother to Nanny's house. Joe raced home from work, and we took the body to the vet. I needed someone official to tell me because I simply could not believe that my boy was really gone. Young, healthy, beautiful Jai was dead. *My Shooting Star*, I called him. He burned so briefly and so brilliantly.

The loss of Jai has been perhaps the greatest heartache in my life. Jai's death was also, in part, one of the things that set me on the path toward becoming a professional animal communicator.

It was in that capacity that a dear friend in Michigan, Amy, contacted me. She had bred her saluki, Zahrah, to a handsome and impressive male, Boss. She asked me to touch in with Zahrah to see if the lovely lady would tell us whether she was pregnant.

I contacted Zahrah, and her first words to me were, "So, are you taking a puppy?" It was a totally unexpected question. I told her "No," but apparently I was wrong.

Not long after that, Jai started trying to get through to me from the world of spirit. Even though I've frequently communicated with animals who have passed on, I had not done so with Jai. Each time I tried, the pain would be too great, and I would block the connection. Now he was nudging at my thoughts, trying to get in, and asking me to listen. He wanted to come back. I knew through the contact with Jai that Zahrah already knew about it.

Still, I didn't trust myself. Another animal communicator, my friend Janice, did a session with Jai, which confirmed what I was getting. He also shared other things with Janice—things she had no way of knowing—including a reference to the "major and minor stars," which Janice asked me to clarify.

When my first saluki, Yoda, died, the star Sirius (heart star of Canis Major) shone through my bedroom window, comforting me through a long, sad winter. I imagined Jai together with Yoda, and the natural progression of this thought was to associate Jai with Procyon, the heart star of Canis Minor. They were my two dog stars.

Jai also told Janice he would be dark in color, as well as some other details that we were to watch for, such as a marking of significance.

When I told Amy what Janice had said, I thought I might be met with some skepticism. In contrast, Amy appeared to be waiting for such news. She was thrilled and felt it fit right in with the things she had been feeling from Zahrah.

Zahrah had four black and five sable pups on July 21, 2002. All the sable pups were girls. The blacks were three boys and a girl. Puppy number eight was a little black boy, the smallest of the three, named Kai. He was obsessed with getting to Amy, the breeder, rather than to the milk bar with his siblings. He would follow her, moving as she did and heading toward her as if on a mission. Finally, she picked him up and told him, "It's okay, Kai, I know who you are." Then he settled down and nursed.

As Kai grew to the ten-week age of adoption, various indications surfaced that he indeed was Jai returned. One sign was his "significant marking." Amy took a photo of him standing with his front feet on a box, a black puppy with tan and white points. The white on his little chest reminded me of a bird. Then a friend of Amy's asked, "Who's taking the black puppy with the rising phoenix on his chest?"

Not long after the pups were born, I went out to Jai's grave and was met by a shocking sight. The writing on the headstone was gone. It had been fading a bit, but it was still readable the last time I'd looked. Now it was gone.

The headstone is made of slate.

A clean slate.

The most amazing moment, however, came as we finally arrived home on September 29, Kai's ten-week birthday. We'd been driving for fourteen hours, traversing the long distance from Grand Rapids, Michigan, to Middleburgh, New York. We took the puppies out of the car and into the backyard. As I set Kai down in his new yard for the first time, at least the first time for this set of feet, I happened to glance up. As Kai's little feet touched the earth of his new home, a brilliant meteor streaked across the night sky.

My *Shooting Star* was home.

We have had some other physical proof phenomena about Kai being Jai returned. Kai developed a pattern of freckles on his chest that reflected the constellation Canis Major. In addition, he and Jai are the only dogs of any breed I've ever known who respond to catnip like a feline.

Be on the lookout. You may notice patterns or guiding details about your animal friends that confirm their previous existence with you as a particular animal family member.

🐾 DETAILED INSTRUCTIONS 🐾

Sometimes animals give specific, stunning details of how and where to find them in their new reincarnated form. Here are a few intriguing and even humorous examples of how some animals spelled out their return or worked out intricate details to harmonize with their human companions. Animal communicator Diane Samsel got meticulous instructions from a client's cat about his return.

When Kelly McGowan called me, she was crying hysterically. She had just come home to find Junior, her three-year-old gray cat, dead in the street in front of her home. Kelly's vet had given her my number and told her to please call me.

Junior was quite matter of fact: "I didn't like my body. There was something wrong with it that you didn't know about, and there's a new body for me a few miles from here. Please go get it."

Junior then gave me explicit directions for Kelly: "Turn left from the driveway and travel three miles. You'll see an abandoned barn on the right. Turn right there onto the dirt road. Travel one mile and you'll see a white farmhouse on the left. There's a sign in the yard that says they're giving away kittens. I'll be waiting."

Kelly was dazed and a bit skeptical, but she said goodbye and headed out. Forty five minutes later she called me, the most excited woman I've ever heard. "Diane, I've got Junior!"

She had followed the directions, found the landmarks, come to the little white farmhouse with the "free kittens" signs, and there, nestled in a box, was an eight-week-old gray kitten, the image of Junior!

Sue called Jacquelin Smith to ask her to communicate with her cat, Ming, who had transitioned from her body a few nights before.

Ming said, "I'll be back in six months, and this time I'll be taking the body of a little dog. Tell Sue she can find me in a place she wouldn't ordinarily go and that I'll have a white star on my forehead. She'll know me when she looks into my eyes. We still have lessons to learn together."

Sue doesn't usually go into pet stores, but six months later she happened to walk into one. As she looked around the store, she saw a little dog with a white star on her forehead. Sue called me and said, "When I looked into her eyes, I knew it was Ming."

Animal communicator Nedda Wittels was asked to speak with a family's cat, Milo, who was sick and getting ready to leave her body. After she passed, they spoke again. Milo was eager to return and had definite ideas about it.

"I never liked my name," she said. "I want to be female again, but I want a feminine name this time. Also, I want to be a dog. I haven't been one before and would like to try it out. If I come as a small dog, I can still sit in your lap and get cuddled like I used to. A small, fluffy, lap-sized dog is what I would like to be, probably white in color."

The woman I was speaking with was excited about Milo's plans to come back. However, she had a request. "My husband and I have been talking about getting a dog, so I think this could work out," the woman said. "But I know my husband wants a larger dog, like a golden retriever. Milo, are you willing to come back as that kind of dog? You wouldn't fit into a lap when you were fully grown, but you could come on hikes with us and play all sorts of games."

Milo thought about it. "Well," she said, "I guess I could be a golden retriever, but I want to be a light color."

"Golden retrievers can be a pale shade of gold that is nearly white," I told Milo. She agreed that this would be acceptable.

When we next checked in with Milo, my image of her was that of a small puppy. She was getting ready to inhabit a tiny puppy body, and that's how I saw her in my mind. The woman asked me how to find Milo, and I assured her that she would recognize Milo's energy. "Just start looking for golden retriever puppies pale gold in color. Milo's energy and spirit will feel the same. Look into her eyes, and you will probably know her immediately."

I didn't hear from the client again. Then one day, I was speaking with the person who had referred Milo's family to me. "They found

Milo," the woman said. "They knew immediately. She is a beautiful, pale gold color, and everyone is happy to have her back home. They named her Sally. She learned her name immediately and really likes it."

🐾 ALL OUR RELATIONS 🐾

Animals who come back to us may have been former members of our human family, even if they inhabit the animal form only temporarily to complete their task with us. Animal communicator Anita Curtis tells about meeting her deceased mother in the form of a horse.

In January 1994, I took an early retirement package from the large company I worked for in order to devote all of my time to animal communication. I also took a part-time job at an Arabian breeding stable near my house. I cleaned horses and stalls, and did all kinds of odd jobs, which was a far cry from the bustling accounting department I was used to. I loved the change of pace.

I was scheduled to go to Penelope's home for advanced courses in early February. I was counting the hours. One of the mares was due to have her foal and I wanted to be there, but I wanted the course more. I asked the mare, Briana, when she was going to foal. "Tuesday five," she said.

I confirmed, "Tuesday at five o'clock?"

She sighed and repeated, "Tuesday five." No matter what I asked, that is all she would say. I felt like I was annoying her, so I stopped my badgering.

I flew to California, and when I woke up on Saturday, February 5th, I knew Briana had given birth to her baby. I called home, and my husband confirmed that the stable manager had called and said the baby girl had been born about 3:00 AM.

I arrived home a few days later in the middle of a nasty blizzard, but the next morning I was at the barn to admire Briana's beautiful baby. We took to each other at once. She was my favorite color: bay, a mahogany brown with black stockings up to her knees. She had a black mane and tail, and her ears had black around the edges. I bent over, and she raised her little muzzle and touched my lips. I was in love! It did not occur to me to notice that she did not look like the other Arabian foals, but more like the quarter horses I favored. Her hooves were a bit too small for her size, and her neck did not have the usual graceful curve of her breed. She had a funny habit of sucking on her tongue. None of it mattered to me. I thought she was perfect.

Briana asked us to tell her human companion that she would like her baby's registered name to be Legends Desire. He agreed, but we needed a barn name. The stable manager and I were discussing it, when one of the other pregnant mares offered an opinion. Briana and another mare, Porcia, were mortal enemies and had engaged in a nasty battle for the title of Alpha Mare. Porcia was getting tired of the fuss over Briana's youngster, and she knew that "Bint" meant "Daughter of." Porcia got the stable manager's attention and said, "Bint Bitch."

We decided on BB, which could stand for: Briana's Baby or Bint Briana. BB responded to her name, so it stuck.

One day, I started to realize some strange things. BB was born on the anniversary of my mother's death, which was also about three in the morning. My mother was a heavy smoker, and BB's habit of sucking on her tongue reminded me of my mother's habit. My mother's name was Beatrice, and when she was young her family called her BeeBee. And yes, her feet were rather small.

I was used to giving past life messages to clients, but I couldn't believe anything like this could happen to me. I wrote to Penelope and explained the situation. I asked if she had any thoughts about it.

Penelope answered my letter with a question: Had I figured out if this was my mother or someone my mother had sent? The latter made sense. There was quite a bit of unfinished business between my mother and me at the time of her death. She died in my home, and for the next ten years her presence there was quite strong. I finally had someone come in and ask her to leave. Afterwards, the energy in the house was calm. A year later BB came into my life.

I gave Penelope's letter to the stable manager and went to turn Briana and BB out to pasture. They galloped off, and I closed the pasture gate.

BB suddenly stopped running, turned, and trotted back up to [me]. Then she turned her neck to get her head through the poles of the gate, looked me in the eye, and said, "I am she." I was shocked.

Later in the day, I found a quiet spot and meditated. I finally got the answer to "Tuesday Five." My mother died Tuesday, February 5.

Months later, BB was weaned and ready to go to a trainer in another state. She still looked more like a quarter horse than an Arabian, and the owner was not pleased. The stable manager asked the owner if he would sell her to me. He was glad to get rid of what he thought was an ugly duckling. I had just dropped a car from my insurance policy and received a refund. The owner came up with a price that was within a dollar of the check. BB was to be my horse.

My husband was fine with the idea, but my son wanted to know how he should introduce her to his friends! It never became a problem.

BB came to live with us, and later Briana did, too, when the owner went out of the horse business. We loved each other unconditionally, and I felt at peace with her energy. Several years went by, and one day I noticed that BB's personality had changed. I believe my mother had accomplished what she needed to do and moved on in her spiritual journey.

You may never have such complex relationships with your reincarnated animal friends. However, these kinds of experiences can help you understand your past life connections with the beings in your current life.

🐾 FAITH AND TRUST 🐾

Sometimes our journeys to find our former animal friends—assuming they indicate they are going to reincarnate—take us through many states and stages of spiritual growth, requiring a lot of trust in the process.

Laurie Moore, psychologist and author, tells the story of her journey with her cat, Jessie Justin Joy. Her experience illustrates how we can be transported through many levels of trust and faith with the death and rebirth of our animal friends.

I was constantly scared that my cat Jessie's diabetes would take him away from me. I worried he would not be here for as long as I needed him. I never felt entirely secure, and then one night my boy disappeared.

I called animal communicator Gina Palmer to help locate Jessie. According to Gina, coyotes had attacked him. The next day, I spoke to Annette Betcher, another animal communicator.

Jessie laughed and said to Annette, "I think I may have used up my ninth life."

Annette explained that Jessie wanted to come back to me in a new body.

The many adventures of healing I had with my beloved Jessie flashed before me. A week after he moved in, the vet informed me Jessie had hepatitis, diabetes, a broken pelvis, parasites, a sore throat, a missing toe on an unhealed foot, and the need to have half of his colon removed in order to live. I had specifically told the SPCA staff that I would need to bring him back if he turned out to be ill. Having lost my mother several years before, I desired a long-lived cat. But the universe had other plans in store for me. Avoiding loss was not an option. Finding eternity was.

It dawned upon me that I had been praying for my boy's body to be fully healthy. After six thousand dollars for Western medical operations, Eastern remedies, herbs, trials with special diets, and daily insulin shots, he was much better off but still suffering physically. If Annette was right, perhaps my dream for Jessie's health was going to come true in an unexpected way. Perhaps my prayer was being answered.

I felt Jessie everywhere in my house. I tried to be happy for his spiritual presence, but I was in a state of profound despair and distrust of spirit. Jessie's body being missing left me weeping from my belly. Simultaneously, a new kind of wonder was growing inside of me. Something new was being nurtured, even though my habits of thought and worry were still speaking frequently in my mind.

Five weeks later, Jessie, via Gina, informed me that he could enter a new cat body if I picked one out. This was too much for me to believe. I needed some reassurance. I called Gina three times. I called a psychic. I called another cat intuitive. They all said Jessie loved me and was coming home.

I checked my phone messages and one went like this: "My name is Stacey Caldwell. I live at the end of your street. I don't have your cat, and I'm sorry you lost him. I received your missing cat notice in my mailbox. I have five kittens that are all five weeks old. Would you like one?"

The word "No!" reverberated in my mind. Nobody but Jessie would do. Then it dawned on me. Jessie trying to get through to me because he was coming back. He had reincarnated in a neighbor's house to make it easy for me to find him. Jessie got her to call me, so when I returned her call and she confirmed that two of the kittens were tiger-striped, I was sure I was on the right track.

I'm the kind of person who ends up with a cat in my lap wherever I go. They love me. How can I explain this reincarnation business to the woman? I'll just tell her cats like me. When Jessie runs straight to me, she'll be surprised and delighted that her kitten has found his new human mother. If I mention reincarnation, she might think I'm crazy, or maybe she'll feel sorry for me and assume I'm making it up to avoid the grief. But maybe she'll believe me. Most important of all, she will know which cat is for me because Jessie will run to me immediately.

I arrived and the cats ignored me.

"They haven't met a lot of people yet, so they're shy," Stacey said, apologizing. I approached them, and they ran to all four corners of the living room.

I walked home alone, bending a little more with each step, thinking, "It was the wrong phone call. Someone thought they could help and meant well, but it wasn't Jessie. That's all. He *will* be back. This stuff is all new to me, so I'll listen to my inner feelings more closely."

Intuition sent me back to the place I had first met Jessie. I woke up excited and was at the SPCA early in the morning. So were five other people. Four of us wanted a cat. One of us had five cats to give away. I could feel resolution in my bones. A posted sign indicated that the SPCA was no longer open on Mondays. Well, then it must have been divine intervention. I suggested that all of us follow the man with the five cats to his home and pick one out. He agreed.

As I drove, nothing felt right. I was tired. I missed the turn. My inspiration felt false. "Why can't this be the day?" I screamed inside. "Please just bring me to Jessie!"

We got to the man's house, but the mother cat and her kittens had all disappeared. He took down our names and phone numbers, and promised to call us when they returned. He never called.

I was so angry.

Later, I vaguely felt what was going on within me, deeper than my emotions. With my next breath, curiosity about this life adventure filled me. No longer lost in thoughts of desperation, I had been lit like a campfire and was completely intrigued.

The next morning, I followed a lead from a friend to call another psychic, who could supposedly tell me exactly where a person or thing was located. He was quite pricy, but if he could do the job, he'd be worth it. His voice was stern. His name was Carmel. He told me to go twenty feet northwest and three steps south. He assured me, "The cat will be right there."

We used the compass. His directions led me to a trash bin. It was empty. I called Carmel back but he never returned my call.

I informed Gina, "I am thinking twice about this reincarnation business. I think it's time I just let go. Maybe he's not really dead. Maybe this coyote story is made up. Maybe Annette, Gina, and I are experiencing "multiple shared delusion disorder" under all the stress. I don't know what to do."

I called Annette, who explained that Jessie said he needed to reincarnate in a big male body—no kittens.

I returned to the SPCA and found a beautiful smoky black cat named Shadow. He had arrived the day after Jessie left and had been living there for five weeks. He was the number one favorite of the staff, who couldn't figure out why nobody swooped him up immediately.

Annette relayed Jessie's wishes. "He doesn't need to be tiger-striped. Just make sure he's a big male and that you have an affinity for him."

However, when I spent some time with Shadow, he was not like Jessie at all. Not Jessie's vibe. Not Jessie's soul. Not his eyes.

Nevertheless, when I called Gina and Annette, they confirmed that Jessie would be switching bodies with Shadow once I brought him home. Unexpectedly, a deep rumbling laughter as big as the New York City Central ran through me. The person my feelings were becoming and the person my mind kept thinking had detached from each other. I no longer understood who I was.

Friday afternoon, one hour before closing, I headed to the SPCA to pick up a cat named Shadow. Halfway there, I thought I was losing it and started to turn the car around. It would be too devastating when it didn't work. I believed in magic, but this seemed impossible. I should go home, but what did I have to lose? I raced up the highway with eighteen minutes to spare before the SPCA closed for the weekend. "Leap of faith" made sense now.

Heading home in the soft gray interior of the car, I felt my cat's soul near me but not in Shadow's body. Shadow was nothing like Jessie. I prepared myself for months of Jessie lingering bodiless in the air, while I took care of a kind, warm cat with whom I had no deep connection.

When we arrived home, Shadow immediately dove under the bed. His black and white fluffy body looked handsome against the white comforter behind him. I prepared myself for life with a quiet cat unlike my Jessie Boy, the talker. The air stretched thin with my disappointment.

Four hours later, Shadow began to turn into Jessie right before my eyes. He purred, turned in a little circle, and plopped his back firmly against my chest and face to nap, just like Jessie. His initial timidity was turning into Jessie's strength. As Shadow, he was taciturn and cautiously looked around. As Jessie, he was in charge without needing an invitation. His eye contact changed dramatically to resemble Jessie's. His fear of noises turned into Jessie Boy's courage. He even hissed at a big animal he saw outside.

Soon he rubbed my cheek with his. Jessie Boy was incarnating, far more himself than I had expected. I felt the deepest eternal space of endless love and peace I had ever encountered. We were in another realm for hours.

I thought, "It's angelic. It's bright. It's sweet. Everything is taken care of. My cat is showing me that heaven on Earth is possible. I am formless and timeless, and One Love merged with Jessie."

The eyes that once held Shadow's soul filled up with Jessie's adoration. I recognized my Jessie. He looked into my eyes for an hour, filling me with warmth and expansive sweet energy. My heart was wide open and I no longer had doubts.

Twelve hours later, Jessie Justin Joy (his new name) began to demonstrate his old quirks. A nip on my ankle meant the food was not acceptable. It must be Savory Bits or nothing. He was a master soccer player just like last time. He used to jump behind the desk to unplug the computer when I spent too much time working. In his new body he wasn't as large and didn't have the strength, but he showed me he was trying.

My feline companion was fully Jessie, but his energy was even more powerful. He filled me with light. The couch felt like marshmallows. My thoughts, often jagged and uneven, became velvet sounds.

Friends came over and also recognized that our boy was back with a new body.

A month later, my feline angel and I had a graceful, easy cheer about us. He made it clear he would not be going to the vet. I could call Dr. Blake, the homeopathic vet, but no car rides to the animal clinic, where he had spent too much time during his last incarnation. This time, his body was fully healthy.

Jessie keeps me on track, quieting my restless mind with strong presence. He puts his paw gently on my face. He licks my hand. He massages my head. Jessie looks deeply into my soul and sees me. He is my helper, my friend, and my teacher. He is far more evolved than I, so I tune into him and go to realms of bliss.

Jessie inspires me to discover that real joy includes all circumstances as they are. Inner joy is not dependent upon life being one way or another. It's a feeling of unconditional love for all that is. I am discovering that I can be happy just because I was made to be so. No specific reason is needed.

My cat came back and brought a part of myself with him—a part I must have left behind many years ago. I know I will have my friend with me forever. There is no abandonment to fear. I trust the magic of the universe.

Animals make soul transfers to adult animal forms with the agreement of the current residents. They don't necessarily need to find a newborn body to reincarnate. It seems to be much easier to do this with animal forms than with human bodies because of the difference in socialization and the ability of animals to retain awareness of self as soul essence.

Finding our animal friends who intend to come back to us in another physical form stretches us to trust our intuition and practice our ability to connect and follow what we know. When we act out of fear and lack of trust, we can become lost in desperation and confusion, and scatter in directions that lead to more desperation. Taking time to be quiet and find the center of our being, where all is calm and we can connect deeply with others, is necessary in order to grow in our ability to communicate with animals in spirit. What an amazing journey of discovery of life and ourselves we take when we begin to realize who animals really are and what they can teach us.

🐾 HELPING US GROW 🐾

As we have discussed, animals often return as our teachers and soul friends, and continue to guide us. Kazuko Tao tells the story of why her cat returned to her, and the valuable lessons she learned through several of her cat's lifetimes:

> I found Samhain as an abandoned kitten in a schoolyard when I moved to California about sixteen years ago. This feline is fiercely independent, likes to be alone, and clearly states her limits and boundaries at all times. She lives her life quietly and with focused intention.
>
> After living with her for some time, I began to feel Samhain was familiar. It was as if we'd known each other before. I asked her if we had met in another life, and she confirmed that she was the orange cat I adopted during my elementary school days in Japan.
>
> My mother did not like cats, yet having one was important to me. The first animal I loved as a small child was a cat. We used to play hide and seek for hours. So, despite my mother's disapproval, one day I

brought home an orange kitten. Although it was tense between my mother and me, she allowed me to keep the kitten because both my sister and brother also loved it. A few months went by and then, suddenly, I couldn't find my little orange cat anywhere.

I was heartbroken and never had another cat until I was grown and on my own. When I asked Samhain why she had disappeared during that life, she said there was tension in our house. She thought it would be best for everyone if she left, so she found another home.

In this life, Samhain continued her habit of leaving when any situation became too tense. She has never gotten along comfortably with my other cats. When she was younger, Samhain would often leave home for days at a time. I'd trek to her hangout by the river to retrieve her.

One winter, she disappeared for six months. I thought I lost her again, but just when I was packing up to move to a new home, Samhain peeked out from behind a tree. She'd survived all those months by hunting. I coaxed her closer and was able to take her with me to our new place.

Several years ago, my now elderly mother came to live with me. She knew I'd been sharing my life and home with many cats. Samhain lived in the granny unit because of her dislike of my other cats. So when my mother moved in, I gave her no choice but to live with Samhain in the granny unit. This time, I decided, Samhain would not leave because of my mother. If anything, my mother would have to leave if she couldn't handle my cat! This was my home, and I was determined to keep my family together.

Surprisingly, my mother gradually began to appreciate and respect Samhain. This feline made her way steadily into my mother's heart and even her bed. The first year, Samhain slept in a bed my mother prepared for her on the floor. The second year, she slept on the foot of my mother's bed. After that, Samhain slept right next to my mother's face. Because my mother is often alone, it's comforting to have a cat companion, and Samhain has been patient with her. Now, my 95-year-old mother and my frail 16-year-old cat can be found watching television side by side on the couch.

Samhain is one of the major forces in helping me find a new level of relating to my mother. My mother and I have always had a difficult relationship. I couldn't let go of our long, emotionally painful history. However, Samhain, the same kitty who left to find a better home during our early years, is now teaching me lessons on forgiveness and letting go. In her own quiet, subtle, yet unmistakable way, Samhain helps me forgive my mother and see that she couldn't offer me what she never had to give. Only at this point in my life am I able to assimilate the lessons my mother has to offer.

Samhain gave me this advice: "Be more spacious. Your energy and soul are huge in comparison to the issue you have with your mother. You have proven to yourself what you are capable of and that is enough. All you need is to know and live the path you have chosen. This is all that matters. Remember you are like a huge stadium and the issue with your mother is ant-sized in comparison. So you should relax, enjoy what you have that enriches your life and speaks to your soul."

When I asked Samhain why she stayed such a short time with me in her previous life as the orange cat and why she came back to me now, she replied: "Even for a short while, I wanted to be with you and have fun. I wanted to give you simple, genuine love. It seemed to me you were lacking in simple loving in a way that was safe for you. You lived with a lot of fear stemming from your father's drinking.

"Now, it's about forgiveness, letting go of old hurts, and standing your ground. I am a living example of all these things. I came back because the time and circumstances were right for you to learn these lessons; they're important lessons for you.

"We go back many lifetimes to when you were a young boy studying in Tibet. I was one of the temple mice, and I used to come by while you were in meditation and tickle you. I also used to come to you when you were reading ancient texts. I kept you company. We go back many thousands of years. I am one of your main guides to assist you. I want what everyone wants: deep connection and love."

We may find in the vast complexity of human relationships over time that our spirit friends in animal form have helped us again and again. What would we do without them?

🐾 FALLING IN LOVE AGAIN 🐾

Many people feel they can never have another animal companion after their beloved animal friend departs. They may feel they can never go through the loss again, that it would be a dishonor to the memory of their friend, or they would do injustice to a new animal by unfavorably comparing him to the departed one. In most cases, after you face your feelings, honor them, and let go of guilt about animal illness and death, it's easy and healthy to create love, joy, and abundance with new animal companions. Your animal friends in spirit may even help you in this process.

Deborah called me many times because her beloved shitzu dog, Charlemagne, was dying. It was a big blow, and she said she'd never have another dog. She kept in contact with Charlemagne in spirit, and he sent his love and joyful light to take care of her. Deborah wanted to know if he would come back. He said not for awhile. He had work to do in the spiritual realm, but he did not want her to be alone.

Although Deborah swore she couldn't replace him, a friend suggested they go and see a litter of shitzu puppies. Once she was with the puppies, she couldn't resist their charm. She had a terrible time choosing and ended up with three of them. She asked me what Charlemagne thought of this, thinking he might be upset. He was so pleased and twinkled mischievously from behind her shoulder. Deborah needed three dogs to replace him because no one individual could do the job.

Janet was heavily mourning the loss of her old Doberman, Cheeta, when her new dog, Rasha, arrived. Janet felt Rasha helped her through her pining. The new dog proceeded to knock the box of

Cheeta's ashes off the shelf and then looked at Janet and said, "Get out of it. I am here. Stop this nonsense."

Matthew wrote after his dear cat had died:

> And though we had planned not to get another cat for at least six months, the phone rang last Tuesday on behalf of a soon-to-be homeless feline. The former "Spike," now rechristened "Raja," has been comfortably ensconced here for three days, and we have all fallen in love with each other.

The animal who has departed often sends another animal companion of whatever kind you need, especially when they themselves are not scheduled to return right away. Sometimes they send a close friend who is a lot like them to help you expand your experience of life, or it might be someone totally different in personality, breed, or species.

I regard my animal companions as some of the most wonderful beings in the universe. However, I have met thousands of fantastic animals. There are so many animals who are looking to share love with people. No one can replace beloved friends because they are unique. However, there are countless wonderful animal beings on Earth to have as new friends. It will soften your loss to connect with good beings of whatever species. Your heart and vision can then expand to include more of the beauty and wholeness of the universe, and you will attract exactly the companionship you need.

10

Contacting Your Animal Friend in Spirit

Live life fully, love yourself more, find bliss, and help others. This is the type of answer that departed animals give when people ask them, "What can I do to honor your life?"

—Kat Berard

When you are in the throes of emotion from the loss of a friend, it may be hard to relax and softly open in order to connect in spirit. Give yourself time to feel your emotions and your process, and to get the support you need from your friends and family (human and non-human) for your tender journey.

I'd like to offer a meditation exercise to help you get in touch with your departed animal companions. When you feel ready, have a friend read the exercise to you, or record it and follow along with the recording.

In doing this exercise, you may or may not make contact the first time. It depends on your readiness to be open to the contact and the animal's availability. Most animals who were close to you will gladly connect and communicate when you are receptive and ask, but sometimes they cannot connect with you at that time. They may be in the middle of their own process of transition to the spirit realm. Honor your intuitive awareness and try again at another time when it feels right.

Sit or lie down comfortably and quietly in a place where you will not be disturbed. You may wish to have a photo or memento of your departed animal companion with you as you do this meditation. You can play some peaceful music, or if you are outside, let the wind in the trees, the birds singing, the dogs barking, or the other sounds guide your attunement with your surroundings. Let the sounds or silence around you help connect you to the Earth in that moment.

Feel your connection to Mother Earth through your feet on the ground or your whole body sitting or lying down. Feel how the Earth holds you in loving support.

Now, breathe deeply and calmly, letting go of any tension you feel in your body as you breathe out. As you continue to breathe slowly and deeply, notice your body. Feel for any tension in your head and let it go as you breathe out. Notice your neck and shoulders, and your arms and hands. Let go of any tightness as you slowly let out your breath.

Feel your back and chest, belly, hips, and buttocks, and release any uncomfortable sensations. Move your awareness through your legs, feet, and toes, and fully let go. Feel yourself breathing peacefully, fully relaxed and tenderly connected to Mother Earth.

If at any time during the meditation you get worried or anxious, go back to the awareness of your breathing and let go of the troubled feeling as you exhale.

Now, picture your departed animal friend as you knew him on Earth, in his elder years or perhaps as a young animal. Picture him joyful and bright, and willing to communicate with you. Let yourself be open to his presence.

Feel your heart opening and connecting to your animal friend in spirit. Let your animal friend, now in spirit, enter your open heart and contact you. Feel her energy. Feel her presence. Let yourself be aware of how close or distant she feels. Feel a circle of communion connecting and surrounding the two of you. Allow yourself to feel, express, and release any emotion that comes up.

When you are relaxed, with your heart and mind open and receptive, sense whether your animal companion would like to give you a message. Accept it in whatever form it comes, perhaps as a thought, a feeling, a sensation of warmth or energy, a verbal message, or a sense of simply knowing what he wishes to convey to you. Acknowledge his presence and communication. Feel his closeness. Allow yourself to be open to engaging in conversation with your animal friend.

Ask any questions you wish of your animal companion—perhaps about how she is doing now, any questions you have about her death, and any thoughts about her experience of the spiritual dimension. Ask about her plans for the future and whether she will reincarnate or come back to you in some form. Imagine that you can receive the answers to your questions from your animal friend and are receiving them now.

Be open and relaxed as you listen attentively through all your extended senses. Breathe deeply. Let go of any anxiety about receiving answers. Take your time and accept whatever feelings, connection, or communication comes to you. If you are not aware of any contact, don't pressure yourself to experience it. You may need to grieve further and express your emotions before you can be receptive to contact or communication with your beloved animal friend. Your animal friend may still be orienting himself in the spiritual realm and may not be quite ready to communicate. Simply be present with your breath and enjoy the communion of thinking warm thoughts and sending good energy to your animal friend in spirit.

End the exercise when it feels right. Let the feeling of warmth and connection that you experienced during this meditation remain with you. Remember, you can tap into it whenever you wish and continue to communicate with your friends who have gone on.

11

Identity, Individuality, and Oneness

One light. Light that is One though the lamps be many.

—Incredible String Band

*T*here is mystery to the essence of souls: their malleability and their quantity. How do we merge with each other, become individuals, adopt forms, travel from dimension to dimension and place to place? How do we change and yet maintain identity or personality characteristics? How do we return to oneness with all, and how can we be both individuals and one with all the rest of creation?

How does the body, with its individual genetic programming and species patterning, affect the spirit as it reincarnates, and vice versa? How much can we remember from our previous lives and apply to our new forms? How much relearning must take place in becoming familiar with our new bodies?

There are different answers for each life. So much depends on individual awareness and the decisions (conscious or otherwise) that we make about our life paths. I ponder this mystery and understand more each time I experience animal friends returning.

It appears that the essence, or core, of who we are travels intact but adds and subtracts characteristics and even soul parts to suit its evolvement, life purpose, or desire for experience. It's also possible for a soul to live in more than one form or have more than one identity at the same time, or live in alternate parallel realities to our usual physical dimension awareness of time and space.

Spirit encompasses total malleability, infinite wizardry, and complete alchemy. We witness the grand design and are part of it, as well as being its co-creators. We are each woven uniquely into the great Tapestry of Life.

Jacquelin Smith relates a case of spiritual influence on a newly adopted animal stemming from an animal friend in spirit. Denny called Jacquelin to find out about a Doberman pup, Astor, he had adopted six months previously. First, Denny explained that his beloved Doberman, Starburst, had died ten months ago. Astor came into his life through a series of synchronistic events.

Astor had some specific mannerisms, which Starburst had also exhibited throughout his life. Denny felt the mannerisms went beyond the explanation of breed. When Jacquelin communicated with Astor, it was clear that a bit of Starburst's soul had reincarnated with Astor. There appeared to be "mix of spirits" going on. Astor's personality and spirit were present—yet Starburst was also present as the less dominant spirit.

Jacquelin encouraged Denny to treat Astor as Astor, and not as Starburst, but also to recognize, acknowledge, and enjoy the mannerisms brought in from Starburst.

We could also consider this as an example of energetic imprinting of characteristics onto Astor from the information about Starburst in the energy field surrounding Denny and in the home of the former dog. However, it's also common for spirits to be in touch with their human companions and to communicate for a time in this way. The handling recommended by Jacquelin generally harmonizes this type of situation for all concerned.

In my book, *When Animals Speak*, I chronicle in detail the passage of one of my greatest friends in this life, my former Afghan hound Pasha. His life and death were large for me and for all those he touched. I was exalted when he decided to return to me not long after he died.

Buddha Boy was also an Afghan hound, born February 14, 1993, an astrological opposite to the August birth month of his former incarnation as Pasha. He was four months old when he came with me from his birthplace in Idaho to our home in coastal California, north of San Francisco. His personality was warm and loving like Pasha, but he did not have the wild, free-spirited, roguish nature that caused Pasha to race off on independent adventures. I made an agreement with Pasha before he reincarnated that he would stick close to home and me, and not roam. I didn't want the recurrent anxiety provoked by his dangerous wandering ways again. As Buddha Boy, he kept his agreement and curbed his Afghan hound independence to mainly stay close to me and come when I called.

Buddha Boy and I were inseparable and completely in love. Yet, as time went on, I noticed a change in our connection. At first, Pasha's essence was completely present in Buddha Boy. Then Pasha's spirit gradually began to depart. The passion and wisdom that was so much a part of Pasha's essence slowly disappeared. Pasha had returned in the body of Buddha Boy because I needed him so much. Now, he had to continue his soul journey in the spirit realm.

I began to observe Pasha's departure by an estimation of how great a percentage of Pasha's soul presence was melded with the essence of Buddha Boy's spirit and personality. At around two years, Pasha was about 85 percent united with Buddha Boy. By six years of age, his presence was about 20 percent. By nine years, Pasha's essence was gone from the new dog form. He was no longer merged with the spirit of Buddha Boy, sharing his dog nature. Pasha's home was now completely in the heavenly cosmos.

After that time, my relationship with Buddha Boy changed. Buddha Boy as embodied spirit was not the mature, wise, and confident presence of Pasha. While Pasha was a soul mate who looked deep into my eyes, Buddha Boy was more like a little boy who tucked his tail, desperately needing to be loved. He could not meet my gaze for more than a few seconds. Although I loved Buddha, I wasn't deeply in love with him like I had been with Pasha.

We had to find a new relationship with each other. By the time Buddha Boy's life as an Afghan neared an end in the autumn of 2005, we had made peace with the changes that life brings to us all, and we felt a deep, tender love for each other.

🐾 SOUL RETRIEVAL 🐾

Taking our animal friends back into our hearts completely after they have departed physical form can be like regaining a lost part of our soul essence.

Reya was another one of my former Afghan companions. I called her my ray of light. She was a light, gentle, delicately sensitive, and graceful being with the ethereal quality of stardust. I was not aware of having known her in earthly form during previous lives as I was with other animal companions. Then I discovered she had not lived other lives on Earth, as many beings have, but traveled in other dimensions. She appeared in dog form especially to be with me and touch other souls with her grace.

Reya made her exit from this Earth with dignity and the highest spiritual energy. She lay down during the night on a path in our garden. In the full presence of the bright full moon, the Ancient Grandmother spirits escorted her toward the southern sky.

After about a week of feeling her presence large among the stars, Reya's spirit joined with the deepest recesses of my open heart. I felt a part of me had come home from the stars. It was like soul retrieval, gathering a lost part of me that had not come to Earth before. Reya was totally home as a melded life force ray of light forever one with me.

My other departed animal friends dwell in my memory and heart in love. They have individual identities, and they communicate as separate souls with unique missions and purposes as they travel through the spiritual realms and from life to life. But Reya was different. When I looked at her, I felt like I was looking into a mirror at a part of myself. After her death, she melted into my being as liquid silver-gold. I will forever cherish the part of my soul called Reya, who incarnated to give me special grace and then gave me back her total being.

A client of Barbara Janelle relates her experience of soul reunion with her cat, Fudge:

> Fudge was feral when I rescued him, after three dogs had chased him into a stream. It was a joy to win him over and see him blossom in my home. A couple of years later, I was out of the country when he was killed in the lane by a neighbor's car. My first day home, I sat in the living room feeling how much I missed him. When I moved into meditation, Fudge stood clearly in front of me. I watched as he wound himself around me and then melded into the female aspect of my being. Then I understood he was indeed a part of me. We were of the same spirit.

🐾 INTO ONENESS 🐾

The journey of rediscovering how to communicate telepathically with animals parallels what we experience when animal friends in spirit travel from life to death and then back to life again. Both experiences show us how to move from a notion of separate identity and into union with our animal friends.

While I was teaching a Basic Course on how to communicate with animals in Germany in October 1999, the whole process of opening to telepathic communication—and the stages of growth that people travel on this journey from separateness to oneness—revealed itself in a clear sequence.

In learning how to communicate with animals, people usually start out feeling themselves as separate from other species. They see the animals as apart from themselves, in some way objectified. They feel they cannot communicate with animals, or only in a limited way. Direct two-way communication feels foreign. They use their minds to try and figure things out about animals instead of directly receiving feelings and thoughts from the animals. At this stage, they hope they can learn how to telepathically communicate with animals, but they are usually not certain about the possibility.

As people start to open to telepathic reception, they feel their own blocks, inhibiting structures, restrictions, internal cages, conditioning, pain, and suppressed emotion. At this stage of separateness, they often project onto others through their own filters, agendas, and unconscious motives. They may be so locked into their own defensive patterns and identities that they have a hard time truly feeling or perceiving anyone or anything, even themselves.

As they persist in the desire to communicate, and practice getting beyond their own barriers, they begin to receive morsels of true telepathic communication from animals. Because of their inexperience in recognizing how telepathic communication works and feels, they are usually unsure whether it's the animal's thoughts and feelings they are receiving or their own projections. By learning to trust their own process and acknowledging the perceptions they receive, they start to feel the sensation of true telepathic reception within themselves, as opposed to the manipulation of projection. They begin to sense the difference between the thoughts and feelings of the animals and their own. The animals are usually happy to validate true reception by showing their positive response that the person has indeed understood them. People begin to believe that telepathic communication is really happening for them, but they may still have doubts about how well they can do it.

Telepathic reception is a connection through both the heart (feelings) and the mind (thoughts). Our culture's educational system emphasizes mental processes over intuition, thinking over feeling, and head over heart. Often, beginning students open first to the mental part of telepathy. They may more easily receive telepathic communication in the form of mental messages or verbal thoughts. They may also tend to add their own thoughts to the animal's communication as they translate or interpret the mind-to-mind message.

As people continue to open, soften, feel, and receive more through their heart and whole body, they get more of the full range of telepathic communication from animals, including the animal's feelings, emotions, and physical sensations. At this stage, people can still easily distort the communication with the addition of their own emotional agendas. However, as they practice the communication process, they learn how to recognize and accept the purity and simplicity of what they get from the animals.

As students learn to quiet their minds more and face the personal blocks or agendas that get in the way of clear telepathic reception, they receive more of the complete, true communication from animals. Their own defenses melt with the assistance of the acceptance, validation, and compassion the animals invariably communicate. They heal themselves as they open to receive more communication. Their own reception channel gets wider and clearer.

As students advance using the guidance of courses and their own practice, they learn repeatedly from communication with other species, and even other members of their own species, that all ways of being, no matter how different from their own, are okay. As they experience more acceptance of their dark side, including previously unacceptable traits or "un-owned" aspects of being, they move into more openness and the ability to be and feel others as one—as aspects of self.

The deep compassion that animals have for us as human beings helps us learn to accept ourselves as we are. Loving compassion for others and self grows. The communication channel becomes more open, and reception becomes easier and clearer. It becomes easier to feel what animals are feeling, sensing, and thinking. There is less and less artificial separation. The distance is bridged. Communion flows into oneness with the animals and deep-felt understanding for all of life.

At this stage, people know with certainty that telepathic communication is real, and they understand more of its complete nature. Then an amazing, mind-boggling state begins to be experienced. The communication and connection expands into the *One Pool of Openness, where all thought and feeling is One.* It doesn't matter who is originating the question or answer. *The One Wisdom is heard and the One Love is felt in one's being, which encompasses all beings.*

As a person relaxes into and sustains this all-encompassing openness, others around that person reflect it and open more to who that person really is. On the path of spiritual growth, others reflect a person's restrictions and areas that are crying for healing and growth, and echo them back in thoughts, feelings, and behavior. Thus, we attract other humans and other species who highlight in their own being what we need to work on.

The deepening process of telepathic communication often shows us where we are stuck, causing confusion and upset. It takes continual work on ourselves to become clear, open channels of oneness, peace, and deepest love.

Breathe, soften, relax, feel your feet on the Earth, and connect. Use the means that work for you to feel the connection with self and others until it blends more consistently into noneffort—into union. Then all reception, perception, and communication will hold more truth, and you will stand more within your soul center, the source of love and wisdom.

As we learn to celebrate all that we perceive about others and ourselves, instead of judging, criticizing, and struggling, we move from pain into a place of peaceful union within and all around us. All this is possible on the path of connection, our telepathic journey with all of life. Let us celebrate the amazing, joyful, exciting, and adventurous path of awakening that our sisters and brothers of other species open to us.

🐾 ANIMAL DEATH: A SPIRITUAL JOURNEY 🐾

I'd like to share a poetic inspiration that came through many years ago and envisions animal death as a spiritual journey.

Everything is so beautiful, so true upon the Earth, if we but see the abundant harmony and enchantment here. We make it so or make it different.

The woods, the fields, the ocean, the lakes, the rivers, and the streams all cry out for joy in their growing and flowing. See the magic. Feel the grace. See the harmony that renews life and restores grace, even in death, dying, and disease.

Cling not to forms unchanging. See the glory in the dance of form dissolving and resolving. Cease to fight the shifting molecules with orders, chains, tears, and cries of "No, it cannot be."

Flow with spirit, ever-changing in its guises. See the wildflowers bloom and die and give their seeds to the Earth. Nothing ever really dies or fades. Everything dissolves into unity and flows into another sea or shower or puff of air.

Flow your own tears with the tide. Feel your changes. Watch as spirit laughs and, like a blind magician, transforms death, decay, and destruction into rebirth, new growth, and creation abundantly harmonious.

Grind not against the wind, but weave your patterns in the unity of rainbows and melting snow, nourishing the senses and the pulsing, breathing, living Earth.

Be the creator, weaver, magician, and spellbinder that you are, always were, and will be endlessly, even when you, too, dissolve in the light of endless artistry.

Contributors

First of all, I'd like to thank the following authors for allowing me to use passages from their books:

Anderson, Karen. *Hear All Creatures!* (Woonsocket, RI: New River Press) Copyright © 2007 by Karen Anderson. Reprinted by permission of Karen Anderson. www.karenanderson.net.

Brunke, Dawn Baumann. *Awakening to Animal Voices* (Rochester, VT: Bindu Books, a division of Inner Traditions International.) Copyright © 2004 by Dawn Baumann Brunke. Reprinted by permission of Dawn Baumann Brunke. www.animalvoices.net.

Severino, Elizabeth. *The Animals' Viewpoint on Dying, Death, and Euthanasia* (Turnersville, NJ: The Healing Connection) Copyright © 2002 by Elizabeth Severino, D.D., D.R.S. Reprinted by permission of Elizabeth Severino. www.elizabethseverino.com.

Smith, Jacquelin. *Animal Communication* (Lakeville, MN: Galde Press, Inc.) Copyright © 2005 by Jacquelin Smith. Reprinted by permission of Jacquelin Smith. www.jacquelinsmith.com.

Sondel, Nancy R. *Of Wind and Wings* (book in progress). Copyright © 2007 by Nancy R. Sondel. Reprinted by permission of Nancy Sondel.

A huge thank-you to my fellow animal communicators for sharing their life work with me and animal communication clients and students, and for allowing me to tell their tales to the world:

Anita Curtis (www.anitacurtis.com)
Annette Betcher
    (www.annettebetcher.com)
Barbara Janelle (www.barbarajanelle.com)
Barbara Molloy
Betty Lewis
    (http://home.earthlink.net/~pawsreflect)
Catherine Ferguson
    (www.cfergusonconsult.com)
Cathy Malkin-Currea
    (www.animalmuse.com)
Cindy Wenger
    (www.PeaceableKingdomAC.com)
Dawn Baumann Brunke
    (www.animalvoices.net)
Diane Samsel (www.powerpaws.com)
Dixie Golins
Dr. Laurie Moore, LMFT
    (www.AnimalIntuitiveReadings.com)
Elizabeth Severino
    (www.elizabethseverino.com)
Gayle P. Nastasi (www.gazehound.com/pets)
Georgina Cyr
    (www.animal-communicator.com)
Gina Palmer (www.pawsandclaws.net)
Jacquelin Smith (www.jacquelinsmith.com)
Joan Fox (www.animaltalkonline.com)
Joanna Seere (www.spirit-to-spirit.net)

Karen E. Craft (www.AnimalShaman.com)
Karen Taylor (www.SpotSaid.com)
Karina Heuzeroth (www.tiergefuehle.de)
Karla McCoy (www.AnimalTell.com)
Kat Berard (www.katberard.com)
Kazuko Tao, RVT
Marta M. Guzmán
Mary Stoffel (www.humanimal.com)
Michel Sherman
Morgine Jurdan
    (www.communicationswithlove.com)
Nancy Sondel
Nedda Wittels
    (www.raysofhealinglight.com)
Neil Jarrell
Pamela Au
    (http://wingedwolf.citymax.com)
Patti Henningsen
    (www.animaltranslator.com)
Sharon Callahan (www.anaflora.com)
Sondy Kaska
Starr Taovil
Sue Becker
Sue Hopple
Teresa Wagner
    (www.animalsinourhearts.com)
Tricia Hart
Val Heart (www.ValHeart.com)